Bit Players
In The
Big Play

Pamela J. Tinnin
Peter K. Perry
Bass M. Mitchell

CSS Publishing Company, Inc., Lima, Ohio

BIT PLAYERS IN THE BIG PLAY

Copyright © 2004 by
CSS Publishing Company, Inc.
Lima, Ohio

The original purchaser may photocopy material in this publication for use as it was intended (i.e., worship material for worship use; educational material for classroom use; dramatic material for staging or production). No additional permission is required from the publisher for such copying by the original purchaser only. Inquiries should be addressed to: Permissions, CSS Publishing Company, Inc., P.O. Box 4503, Lima, Ohio 45802-4503.

Scripture quotations are from the New Revised Standard Version of the Bible, copyright 1989 by the Division of Christian Education of the National Council of the Churches of Christ in the USA. Used by permission.

For more information about CSS Publishing Company resources, visit our website at www.csspub.com or e-mail us at custserv@csspub.com or call (800) 241-4056.

ISBN 0-7880-2330-6 PRINTED IN U.S.A.

*To the good people in the churches
we have been called to serve,
for their encouragement and willingness
to receive the Good News
in some new ways ...*

Pam, Peter, and Bass

Table Of Contents

Introduction   9
    An interview with the authors on the craft of the first-person narrative

Advent And Christmas

This Way To Bethlehem   23
    by Bass M. Mitchell
    A readers' theater dealing with the passages about John the Baptist as the forerunner of the Messiah.

Herod — The First Christmas Grinch   33
    by Bass M. Mitchell
    Matthew 2:1-2, 8, 16-18
    A readers' theater of various characters, including Herod, tell of the events surrounding the birth of Jesus.

Leaving Egypt For Home   45
    by Pamela J. Tinnin
    Matthew 2:19-23
    Some time after fleeing to Egypt, Joseph dreams it is safe to return to Israel. Mary, the young mother, finds herself strangely sad to leave, wondering what lies ahead.

The Life And Ministry Of Jesus

Never Too Late   53
    by Pamela J. Tinnin
    Matthew 3:1-12
    A young girl meets John the Baptist and faces the questions we all face — will we truly repent and choose the way of Jesus? Is it ever too late?

My Name Is Levi 59
    by Peter K. Perry
    Mark 2:13-17
        The tax collector Levi, who becomes Matthew, tells his story.

Living Water 65
    by Pamela J. Tinnin
    John 4:7-30
        A woman tells of the struggles and trials of her life and of how a seemingly chance encounter with a man at a well brings new life and salvation.

Kneeling Before Him 71
    by Pamela J. Tinnin
    Luke 10:38-42
        A neighbor woman and good friend of Mary and Martha tells how each chose their own way to honor Jesus.

Holy Week And Easter

Just A Jar Of Water 77
    by Peter K. Perry
    Luke 22:7-13
        A Maundy Thursday story from the man in whose house Jesus and his disciples celebrated the Passover in the Upper Room.

What Is Truth? 83
    by Pamela J. Tinnin
    John 18:28-38
        An old cleaning woman sees everything that happens the day Jesus is brought before Pilate. She never lets on that she has met the accused man before.

I Have Seen The Lord! 87
    by Bass M. Mitchell
    John 20:1-18
        Mary Magdala as the first witness to the resurrection.

The Early Church Grows

Rock The Boat! 95
    by Bass M. Mitchell
    John 21
        A conversation between the disciples while in a boat.

Even The Gentiles 99
    by Peter K. Perry
    Acts 10 And 11
        Simon of Joppa gives his testimony before the Council of Elders.

Onesimus 105
    by Peter K. Perry
    Letter To Philemon
        Onesimus, the once runaway slave of Philemon, who became a co-worker with Paul, tells his story.

About The Authors 111

Introduction

Notes

An interview with Pamela J. Tinnin, Peter K. Perry, and Bass M. Mitchell in regard to using drama, especially first-person narratives in preaching.

Q: Tell us something about yourselves.

Pam: In August 1996, I arrived as the full-time pastor of Partridge Community Church-UCC, the only church in Partridge, Kansas, population 250. Prior to my 1996 graduation from Pacific School of Religion, Berkeley, California, I was an editor for ten years with the University of California, Berkeley. I had previously worked as the editor of a small-town newspaper and had co-owned and operated a desktop publishing business. Additionally, I was a long-time sheeprancher and a freelance writer of fiction and non-fiction, published in the *San Francisco Chronicle*, *The Shepherd*, and *Sonoma Monthly*. Currently, in addition to my primary role as a full-time pastor, I still do editorial consulting and desktop publishing via the Internet, and am a reporter for a local weekly paper where I am a general news reporter and film reviewer.

In the past, I was a paralegal working with incarcerated clients, a migrant worker in the fields of Oregon, and a grocery store clerk. I live with my husband, Zack, in Cloverdale, California. We have three adult children, one in Kansas, two on the West Coast.

Peter: I am a United Methodist pastor living in Phoenix, Arizona, where I serve as pastor of First United Methodist Church. I am a 1985 graduate of Pacific School of Religion in Berkeley, California. My wife, Karen, and I have two children, David and Betsy, who often take the opportunity to critique the morning sermon from the back seat of the car on the way home from church. I know that if the kids liked it, then the sermon was a success. The all-time favorite sermons have been the narrative sermons that present the gospel message by focusing on a biblical character and allowing for the imaginative interpretation of biblical and historical events to move the story along. My imagination is captivated by the lives of the first Christians. I would have loved to have lived in those days when the church was young and the gospel was new. Narrative sermons help me capture some of that newness of faith for contemporary Christians. When not writing sermons and doing other work at the church, I prefer to "veg" around the house with a good work of fiction, to move dirt around in my backyard, or to visit with good friends. I am interested in photography and computers.

Bass: I, too, am a United Methodist minister presently serving in Charlottesville, Virginia. I did my seminary work at Duke Divinity School and Southeastern Seminary. My wife is Debbie. We have two children, Michael and Meredith. From as far back as I can remember I wanted to be a writer. Over the years I have pursued this dream. I have written lots of articles for various publications, as well as curriculum material for the United Methodist Publishing House. Abingdon Press has published two of my books, *In Every Blade Of Rustling Grass* and *God Sightings*. I enjoy teaching, preaching, reading, hiking, and conducting workshops and seminars on a variety of ministry topics.

Let me add a word about how this book came to be. I have met a lot of friends over the internet, especially through clergy e-mail lists. Having enjoyed doing first-person sermons and using drama in worship, I became aware of Pam and Peter's work as they sometimes shared what they were doing on those lists. The idea came to me that we should get together and combine our efforts. As you can see from this book, many of the wonderful pieces here are from these two extremely gifted preachers and writers. It has been an honor working with them. It's the desire of all of us that these materials inspire you and assist you in your ministry. We offer this book not just for clergy but for lay speakers and church drama teams or anyone interested in innovative preaching and worship.

Q: How would you define this style of preaching demonstrated in these sermons?

Peter: The first-person narrative is an ancient style of preaching and teaching. Some of my favorite Bible stories are, in fact, short examples of this style of preaching. Jesus used the style effectively when he told the story of the man with the barns. "The land of a rich man produced abundantly. And he thought to himself, 'What should I do, for I have no place to store my crops?' Then he said, 'I will do this: I will pull down my barns and build larger ones, and there I will store all my grain and my goods.' And I will say to my soul, 'Soul, you have ample goods laid up for many years; relax, eat, drink, be merry'..." (Luke 12:16 ff).

The first-person narrative sermon is an intimate way of telling a story, as the character essentially holds a conversation with himself or herself. The audience is merely listening in on the conversation, eavesdropping on a life that is in some way touched by God.

Pam: First-person narrative sermons are storytelling at its best. Storytelling is as old as human history. I can easily imagine the early cave dwellers gathered around their fires at night, retelling the excitement and danger of the day's hunt, whether in words or actions or paintings on the wall. When he told stories, Jesus was following an honored and well-known tradition. No offense to those who prefer that particular preaching style, but not once do we read of him preaching a three-point sermon! As someone who has been a storyteller since long before she even knew why, I have come to believe that when we share our stories, we find out new things about ourselves. In the telling and in the sharing of the Good News, we open a window through which the people gathered can see and understand new things about themselves, their lives, their faith. In some holy way, both the teller and the hearers are touched and changed and made new.

Bass: A first-person narrative brings the biblical story and biblical persons to life. They were, after all, real human beings. By placing myself back in their time and in their shoes, I hope to recapture their humanity and their experience of the Good News in a way that will help others experience it, too.

Also, there are not just first-person narratives in this collection. There's a growing popularity today with what some call "readers' theater," in which several persons read various parts. I especially like these because they involve other persons and you can present several different perspectives. Several readers' theater skits are included in this collection.

Q. How did you get introduced to this style of preaching?

Peter: In seminary I was introduced to all sorts of preaching. Since I had a work-study job videotaping all of the preaching classes, I had the opportunity to hear some good preaching, as well as a lot of not-so-good preaching. I videotaped the verse-by-verse exegesis of expository preaching, the call-and-response of African-American preaching, the meandering illustrations of the inductive sermon, the debate style of the dialog sermon, sermons written in poetic meter, topical homilies that often were a proof text of the scriptures, even some sermons delivered silently in clown mime. Of all the sermons I videotaped, however, my favorites were always the first-person narrative sermons of my classmates. These were the biographical sketches based on scripture and imaginatively woven into a story that captured my imagination as I sat behind the viewfinder of the camera. These were the sermons I remembered a week later, or a month later, though now that fifteen years have passed I admit to not remembering the details any more!

Over the years, when moved by the spirit to do so, I have attempted a number of first-person narratives. Often they are rooted in little more than a verse or two of scripture. My reading of history and knowledge of the geography, economics, and politics of the biblical culture allow me to add details. But people haven't changed all that much over the years. The same things that frightened the biblical characters frighten us. The same things that brought joy to a person living in the first century bring joy to us today. And that is why these sermons are so often well received. They may be rooted in the distant past, but they are contemporary. A slave in Ephesus is haunted by his past. So are we. Mary is perplexed by the events in the garden. So are we.

Bass: Unlike Peter, I did not get the benefit of seeing this style in seminary. I'm not even sure it was mentioned. I have seen and read about it, of course, and decided to try it for myself. I was very nervous and still am each time I do it, but the positive feedback I get is really encouraging. It's a style with which everyone, adults, children, and teenagers can readily identify. Our people are into visuals, movies, and stories. So it seems natural to me to share these wonderful stories in such a way. After all, Jesus himself used stories probably more than any other way of teaching and preaching. If it was good enough for him, it certainly is for me.

Pam: I sort of stumbled into it by accident. My first year as a preacher, summer came along with that perennial favorite, Vacation Bible School. While the VBS material wasn't all that bad, each day's program was to include a videotaped storyteller, a woman who was filmed telling that day's story in a rather mundane manner — pretty boring for small children. In desperation, I came up with a character, "The Old Storyteller," who appeared in full costume, limping along with a walking stick, and carrying an old woven bag that held various items (a bit of fishing net, an ancient carving knife, a purple cloth, and so on). While the children loved it, I didn't think too much about it until almost a year later when I was stumped for a sermon. Easter was approaching and suddenly I realized how easily the text (when Pilate confronts Jesus) would lend itself to a dramatic retelling. I've been doing them about every two to three months since then, depending upon whether the lectionary text seems to speak to that style.

Q: What about costumes?

Peter: Some of those seminarians I videotaped in homiletics class so long ago dressed up in character to deliver the sermons. Usually they looked like refugees from last year's Sunday school Christmas pageant. But sometimes, the costume helped to lend some authenticity to the delivery of the message. Just be cautious about using costumes when doing a first-person sermon about Adam or Eve! Personally, I don't use a costume, relying instead upon the imagery of the spoken word to make the character real, even if I am in a three-piece suit or a Geneva robe and Cokesbury stole. For the same reason, I don't try to change my voice in any way. Let the imaginations of your hearers do that for you.

Bass: I agree. Costumes are not essential. You can share effectively without them just by the use of your voice. But do not discount costumes. I have used them before with good results. What we did in our church was have a group of persons volunteer to research biblical costumes and then make them. I use them on occasion but we also use them for other dramas in the church. So I would say to use them if they really enhance your narrative, but don't feel that you must have them for this to be effective.

Pam: Like Peter and Bass, I have found that costumes aren't necessary to "bring a character to life." Usually I don't use them, but under certain circumstances, I believe that just a minor change works to enhance the moment. I sometimes remove my glasses and simply cover my head and shoulders with a black shawl. Whether costumed or not, I suggest keeping it simple. A "suggestion" of a costume is better than trying to recreate a historically correct look. My major exception to this would be with children — they love costumes, the more elaborate, the better, and it only adds to their enjoyment of the experience.

Q: What pointers do you have in how to deliver them?

Pam: While I do not attempt to "fake" an accent, I change my voice slightly and, as with costuming, use that minor change to "suggest" someone from another place and time. Also, trust the material — after all, aren't we sharing the most compelling story ever told, one that has held up these 2,000 years? Besides, if the monologue does what it should, you'll find yourself caught up in the tale — the character will "tell" or "show" you how to speak.

Speaking without notes or a manuscript is almost always the best delivery. However, that's not always possible. I remember the week I had three funerals to prepare! To be honest, mostly I've found that if I don't allow myself to be tied to the manuscript, it can be just about as effective a presentation as one from memory. When you hear your people weeping in despair or laughing in delight, or when that quiet sigh is heard when you step away from the pulpit, you know your story has done its work well.

Peter: Most important in the delivery for a first-person sermon is learning your material by heart. It is hard to be a convincing character if you have to read your own story. But cheer up! Memorization isn't difficult, especially when telling a linear story that you have created in your own mind. For those few moments that you stand before the congregation, you are not the preacher. You are a visitor from far away and long ago, and you have an important story to tell. It is the story of how God once moved in your life. It is the most important story you know. It has made all the difference in who you are. Some things never change.

Bass: Peter is correct. To share the story from memory is most effective. However, it can also be effective to read it, as long as you do not tie yourself to the written text. Look up often. Know it so well that you can tell it without looking at the manuscript too much. I would also suggest this — you do not always have to be the one delivering them. I have recruited several persons in my church who enjoy doing this and sometimes I will ask them to do it. For example, at Easter I had a woman who was actually named

Mary pretend to be Mary, the first person to witness the resurrection. She did a great job. Also, because there are some readers' theater skits in this book, you will need to recruit other persons. Make sure you do so well ahead of time and rehearse it several times. Always speak with enough volume and use good voice dynamics; that is, when a character expresses anger, then sound angry; when joyous, sound like it, and so on. This takes practice, but it really adds to the overall effectiveness. One other point, I always go over it several times on Sunday morning, a couple of times in my study, and then I actually go down to the sanctuary and deliver it once there. I find that this routine prepares me well.

Q: If someone wanted to write their own first-person sermons, what tips would you give them?

Bass: Take a look at some of the ones in this collection. They will give you some ideas about how to go about developing your own. One of the most important things is to do good research. These first-person narratives do use the imagination and we do sometimes have to fill in the gaps of our knowledge, but we do so after a lot of research so that what we say is in keeping with the person, time, culture, and place. After I do the research, I try to put myself in that person's skin, to see, taste, feel, touch, smell as that person would. When I do this, words and images come to mind that I can fashion into a narrative. I also find it helpful to get someone else to read it when finished and give constructive feedback.

Pam: Read the stories in the Bible and let your imagination go. You might find it easier to use a major biblical character as your "voice." Frankly, I try to imagine those "hidden" folks, the ones who are there in the margins if we only look and dream a bit — the servant girl, the next door neighbor kid, the street orphan. I've used the word "suggest" about costuming and voice and mannerisms. Being somewhat of a minimalist, I would say that most important is that ability to "suggest" things as opposed to worrying about each word or phrase or whether you can find authentic Roman armor. In writing the monologue, look for those things that would obviously "stick out" as too modern, but let the story flow naturally.

Peter: The ideas for first-person narrative sermons are not hard to find. We read the scriptures and we know the great stories of faith from Adam and Eve to John on the Island of Patmos. People like Moses, Jeremiah, Peter, and Paul all rise like giants, towering over the Holy Books that contain their stories. But there are countless named and unnamed supporting actors in this great drama of faith. Look for them as you read the text. Imagine how they responded to the touch of God as the heroes of the faith brushed past their lives. We all know about the old woman who gave her two copper coins to the temple treasury. We all know how preachers have used this story to help raise funds for the annual church budget. But what was going through the woman's mind as she looked into Jesus' eyes before sharing her two cents' worth? What was her motivation for giving away everything she had? Where did her two copper coins come from? Had she always been poor? What would she do now that she had given everything to God? The Bible will not answer these kinds of questions, at least not directly. But the preacher who approaches the text prayerfully and imaginatively may discover a great truth that begs to be preached in the story of this widow. First-person narrative sermons are all about imagination. Once your imagination has been piqued with a sense of wonder about a biblical character, the sermon will almost write itself.

In writing a first-person narrative sermon, we try to be faithful to historical truth. I remember walking among the ruins of the ancient city of Gerasa on a tour of the Holy Land early in my ministry, in what is modern-day Jordan. As I strolled down the paved roads among the towering columns, a sermon began to emerge in my mind about the demon-possessed man from Gerasa. Alas, when I got home and checked my commentaries I learned that there are two Gerasas in the Holy Land. The one I visited was not the home of the man whose demon was called Legion. Still, the value of walking where Jesus walked has helped me write many first-person sermons. For in my mind's eye I can feel the hot Mediterranean sun beating down on me, smell the dust under my feet along the highways and byways, taste the sweet fruit from the trees of Jericho, hear the sound of the Jordan River as it babbles by, and feel the cold, hard stone of the walled city of Jerusalem.

Even if you have been to the Holy Land, a good Bible dictionary is still indispensable in the writing of a first-person narrative sermon. Let's say you are reading along in the eighth chapter of the Acts of the Apostles and you come to the story of Simon the magician. Look up the word magician and you learn that the root word is the same one that is used to describe the three Magi who arrived in Bethlehem shortly after the birth of Christ. Hey, maybe Simon was not such a bad guy after all, especially when you consider that he believed Phillip's teachings and stayed with him to see the signs and wonders worked in the name of God. So where did Simon learn his craft? Could it have been from one of the wise men who had come from the east following a star forty years earlier?

Q: What other suggestions or insights do you have to offer in the effective use of this style of preaching?

Pam: As in all preaching, let the Spirit move and then write and speak from the heart. There's no question that first-person narrative sermons are different — it's scary almost every time I attempt one. Then a 16-year-old stops me at the post office and says, "I've been thinking about last Sunday's sermon all week," and it's worth every anxious moment. The hardest part of all is typing those first few words — sometimes I stare at my computer screen for hours and wonder if anything will ever come. Just start typing! Once I have that first paragraph, the story takes off. Like swimming, the only way to do it is to jump in. So come on — the water's fine!

Peter: Some scholars may disagree with me, but I believe that the basic concerns of human beings have not changed all that much since the days when these biblical characters lived. If the sermon you write is addressing the issues that people are most concerned about, then it will be a great sermon! Parents are concerned about children. Youth are concerned about the future. Older folks are concerned about the past. Human beings want to love and be loved. We want to know that our lives have meaning and purpose. We want to know that God is real. Let the characters who grace the pages of your creative efforts speak to these things. Let them wonder what we wonder today.

Bass: Take the risk. This is new and it will take some time to get used to and to do well. But try it anyway. The results are worth it. And it's not a style you will wish to use every Sunday. As Peter says, he uses it when the "Spirit moves" him. When you sense that some passage from the Bible is better shared in this way, then go for it. I use it about three or four times a year.

Advent
And
Christmas

This Way To Bethlehem

by Bass M. Mitchell

Notes
Based on all the readings about John the Baptist in the Gospels.

Characters
Minister
God
John The Baptist
Woman

Props
Costumes would be nice but not necessary
Road signs in the sanctuary that read: Wilderness 12 Miles — This Way To Bethlehem

Scene One:
In The Sanctuary

Minister: Every Advent, Lord, you make us read these words from that strange man who dressed funny and lived out in the desert. I want to be able to say just one year to myself and the people, "Rejoice! Deck your halls with boughs of holly, fa-la-la-la-la." But instead, the message every year is,

John The Baptist: *(Enters, or speaks out of sight)* REPENT! Messiah is coming! REPENT! *(Looks at the Minister and then the congregation, smiles and says)* Merry Christmas! *(Exits)*

Minister: Now see, Lord, that's exactly what I mean. Nobody wants to hear that during the Christmas season. Isn't there a better way to go about this? A more joyous message? Isn't there another way to Bethlehem?

God: *(Speaking over the PA system or hidden from sight the voice of God comes booming back)* No. This way to Bethlehem.

Minister: *(Whining)* But that's through the wilderness.

God: That's right. No way to Bethlehem but through the wilderness.

Minister: But we've got to go to the mall, right? *(Looks to the congregation for support)* We're not ready for Christmas yet. Lots of presents to buy, things to do, you know.

God: Well, on the way to the mall, drop by the wilderness for a visit. There's a man there you need to meet. He can help prepare you for Christmas.

Minister: You mean a jolly old man with a white beard and wearing a red suit?

God: Not exactly. You'll probably smell something like a camel first. Then you'll know he's near, although you'll probably hear him long before you see him. He's a fiery preacher and minister named John the Baptist.

Minister: But, Lord, we really don't have time for a sermon or a Sunday school lesson, do we? *(Looks to the people again for support)* We've just got too much to do. Besides, I'm a preacher myself. If we want to hear a boring sermon, I can always preach one of mine.

God: Well, you've got a point there.

Minister: *(Whining protest)* Hey ... just wait a minute there ...

God: *(Interrupting)* But you'll not find this guy boring. In fact, he'll probably make you angry. Maybe he'll make you think. Just maybe he'll help you, all of you, experience Christmas this year in a way you haven't for a while.

Minister: Okay. I surrender. I'll go to Bethlehem this year through the wilderness. But they *(Points to the people)* have to go with me. And if we don't get all our shopping done, well, we're blaming you.

Scene Two:
In The Wilderness Near The Jordan River

Minister: *(Takes a few steps as if on a journey)* Whew! *(Wipes brow)* This wilderness is really something. I was kind of expecting forests, lakes, that kind of thing. But this isn't a wilderness! This is a desert! It's hot! I don't see a tree in sight, just some scrawny shrubs. How did I let God talk me into this? Man, the mall sure is looking good right now. *(Puts hand above eyes as if looking at something in the distance)* I see something. A river. You see it? *(Referring to the people and pointing to the distance)*

Well, I wouldn't call it a river. More like a muddy stream. And there are people, lots of people standing on the bank. More are coming. Why in the world would so many people be out here? God must have gotten to them, too.

Do you smell something? *(Sniffs the air)* Is that a camel? Man, they smell bad. Look! *(Points)*

Wonder who that is? *(Peers or squints with a fascinated expression)* He's wearing some kind of strange fur coat and a belt tied around his waist. Looks like crude sandals on his feet. I saw people looking like that back in the '60s. His hair is black as a raven. There's fire in his eyes and in his voice.

(Minister walks up beside a bystander — Woman who is also listening intently to John The Baptist. Both Minister and Woman stand listening)

John The Baptist: Prepare the way of the Lord, make his paths straight. Every valley shall be filled, and every mountain and every hill shall be made low, and the crooked shall be made straight; and the rough ways made smooth; and all flesh shall see the salvation of God.

Woman: *(Speaking with a hushed sense of awe)* He's the one.

Minister: The one what?

Woman: *(Reverently)* Elijah.

Minister: The Old Testament prophet?

Woman: Yes. You must know that our scriptures tell us that Elijah will return to prepare for the coming of Messiah. Each year at Passover every family sets an extra place at their table in hopes that the Forerunner, Elijah, the Preparer of the Way, will return. Now he has.

(Woman and Minister look in the distance at John again)

Minister: What's he eating?

Woman: Honey and locusts.

Minister: Honey and what?

Woman: Locusts. You know, grasshoppers. The desert is full of them.

Minister: *(Holds stomach)* Boy, wish I had thought to pack my lunch. Um, I don't suppose there's a McDonald's close by, is there?

Woman: *(Puzzled look)* Huh?

Minister: Oh, nothing. Forget it. What was he talking about just now?

Woman: He was quoting another great prophet, Isaiah, who describes John's purpose and mission. John *is* Elijah –– the Preparer of the Way for the Messiah. This is so exciting!

Minister: But what does he mean by "make the paths straight, fill the valleys"?

Woman: You see, we have a custom. When it's announced that a great king is coming to our village, all the people go out onto the road leading into the village and begin removing rocks, filling potholes, leveling the ground, giving the king a clear path into their town.

Minister: So John's telling everyone to go and clean up the roads?

Woman: *(Laughing)* Not exactly. You're not from around here, are you?

(Minister shakes his/her head and the woman continues)

Woman: Haven't been to the wilderness for a while, either?

Minister: Well, no. I've been kind of busy, you know, with Christmas coming and all ...

Woman: *(Uncertain of pronunciation and meaning)* Chris ... mess?

Minister: Uh, forget it. You were talking about cleaning up the road?

Woman: John's not really talking about roads. He's not telling us to mend the paths to our villages but to mend our hearts, for the King is coming. Messiah is on his way. Whatever we might have in our lives that would keep him from coming in must be uprooted, rolled aside. Nothing must be in Messiah's way.

Minister: But how are you supposed to do that?

John The Baptist: REPENT! Turn away from your sins, for the kingdom of God is near. REPENT!

Minister: Repent? I know that word. I've used it a few times and even experienced it a time or two.

Woman: "Repent" is a very special word in our language. It means much more than to feel sorrow for your sins. Repentance is feeling such sorrow that you turn from your sins; you change the way you live. It's kind of like you are walking in one direction and then suddenly just turn and go in the opposite direction. Repentance is turning from self toward God, from the old life to a new life. Do you understand?

Minister: I think so. But to repent means that you see yourself as a sinner. Isn't that right?

(Woman nods her head and the Minister continues)

Minister: Well, you don't look like a sinner to me. You sure know your Bible. And me, well, I help people all the time, I pray, I read my Bible, I teach Sunday school ...

Woman: You don't really think of yourself as a sinner, then?

Minister: *(Rather grandly)* Well, no. I'm a good person. And all these folks here are good, church-going, tithing people, too. Aren't you? *(Speaks to the people)*

John The Baptist: You brood of vipers! Who warned you to flee from the wrath to come? Bear fruits worthy of repentance. Do not begin to say to yourselves, "We have Abraham as our father"; for I tell you, God is able from these stones to raise up children to Abraham ...

Minister: What does he mean? Who's he talking about?

Woman: Good, synagogue-attending, tithing, Law-abiding people ... See them over there? *(Points and then continues)* All dressed in their fine Sabbath robes. We call them Sadducees and Pharisees. They are quite religious and they don't let you forget it.

Minister: Well, if you ask me, John could sure use a few lessons in how to win friends and influence people. He just called your religious leaders a "brood of vipers," and I don't think it was a compliment. I mean, if *I* preached like that, I'd be sent to the wilderness, too. What did he mean by that brood of vipers stuff anyway?

Woman: You *haven't* been to the wilderness in a while, have you?

(Minister shakes his/her head and Woman continues)

Woman: You see, it is dry here. Sometimes we have brush fires and you can see whole nests of snakes scurrying out from under the bushes, trying to escape. The religious leaders remind John of the snakes — evil, cunning, poisonous — fleeing the fiery judgment God is sending. They're not fooling God, only themselves, for God sees their hearts and their actions.

Minister: What did John mean by telling them to stop calling themselves the "children of Abraham"? That really seemed to upset them.

Woman: They do not consider themselves sinners, so why should they repent? They take great pride in seeing themselves as the children of Abraham. Father Abraham, you see, received great blessings and promises from God, in which they feel that they, too, share. You might say that Abraham had built up such a treasure of merit with God that his descendants could draw upon it for themselves. They believe simply because they are children of Abraham, and not for any merits of their own, that they are safe from God's judgment.

Minister: So what's John really saying to me, I mean, to them?

Woman: He's saying, "If you want to truly repent, stop saying, 'Abraham is our father.' Stop saying, 'My family has always been a member of this church. I tithe.' You are not indispensable to the Lord. God could take stones from this river bed and make them better children of Abraham than you are! God is not interested in your roots. God's interested in your fruits! So stop trying to hide your sins. Be honest with yourselves and with God for a change. Face the truth. Repent and live a life that shows you really mean it. This is the only way to be ready for Messiah's coming."

Minister: But I'm not exactly sure how to do that.

Woman: Look. *(Points)* John may be about to tell you how. See them? *(Points)* Those are tax collectors. Nobody likes them ... the traitors. They want to know what they can do, how they can repent.

John The Baptist: Don't collect more than is legal.

Woman: Now look at that bunch. *(Points)* Roman soldiers. Our people hate them. They lie and cheat and steal from us. But listen to what John says to them.

John The Baptist: Don't take money from anybody by force or accuse anyone falsely. Be content with your pay.

Woman: If *they* can be forgiven, *anyone* can! You see, there are some things we can do. Those tax collectors and soldiers know exactly what they can do. If you think about it, so do you. So do I. I know there are things in my life that I need to repent of, to turn away from, so I can be closer to God, more prepared for God's Messiah. Each of us must look in our own hearts and remove what obstacles we can.

Minister: I believe I'm beginning to understand. John's telling us, "If you really want to get to Bethlehem this year, you've got to come to the wilderness, spend some time looking inside yourself. See your life as a path and identify any obstacles, any roadblocks that would keep the Christ from coming more fully into your life. Then, through repentance, remove it, turn away from it and toward God." Is that right?

Woman: That's right.

Minister: But that's easier said than done sometimes. I mean, I know some people, lots of people, with obstacles and problems they can't move by themselves. We don't have control over lots of things, you know.

Woman: You're right. There are some boulders so large that we cannot remove them on our own. We don't have to. *(Smiles)* All we can do is turn them over to God, ask for God's help, and trust that somehow, in God's own time and way, God will remove them or at least not let them keep us from experiencing the joy and blessings the Messiah brings. And we can help by praying for them, listening, and caring. Remember, with God and good friends, even mountains can be moved.

Minister: You know, you have given me a lot to think about. I believe if someone asks me if I'm ready for Christmas this year that I can actually say I think I am or at least well on my way to being ready ... and I haven't even been to the mall ... just the wilderness.

Woman: There's hope for you yet. Perhaps you should come out to the wilderness more often. It really is the only way to Bethlehem, you know.

Minister: Yes. Now I know.

(Woman and Minister walk off together)

John The Baptist: *(Walks to center aisle)* All of you must get ready. There is One coming after me who is so much greater than I am. I am not worthy even to untie his sandals. He will fill you with the very presence of God. But you must get ready. Turn from your sin and turn to God. REPENT! Messiah is coming. REPENT! *(Starts to walk out, then turns to the audience once again and says with a grin)* Merry Christmas! *(Walks out)*

Herod — The First Christmas Grinch

by Bass M. Mitchell

Matthew 2:1-2, 8, 16-18

Notes
This works well if you have costumes but it's not necessary. I used it both ways and it worked well. You could do without the Narrator or at least some of what the Narrator says if you have costumes or put signs on the readers identifying them. Rewrite as you will. Have at least one practice reading with your group. Cast well. Who's the greatest grinch in your church?

Characters
Narrator
Servant
Herod
Magi
Priest
Angel

Narrator: One day, a group of visitors from the East, Magi, they were called, came to Herod's palace in Jerusalem. They met with the chief servant of the king, who then came before Herod and said,

Servant: Your Majesty, there are some Magi here who wish an audience with you.

Narrator: The king replied,

Herod: What do they want?

Narrator: The king's servant answered,

Servant: I do not know, Your Majesty. They would not tell me.

Narrator: The king mumbled to himself,

Herod: They must be running low on funds for their trip.

Narrator: But the chief servant said,

Servant: Perhaps, Your Majesty, but I sense that they are seeking something else. Should I send them away?

Narrator: Herod rubbed his chin for a moment, wondering if he should bother with them. Finally he said,

Herod: No. Send them in. Perhaps there is something in this for me.

Narrator: The servant left and in a moment he returned with the Magi. One of the Magi, a man with a flowing gray beard, addressed the king:

Magi: Great King Herod, we thank you for seeing us on such a short notice. We know that you are busy with all the good work you are doing in your kingdom. And may God bless you with wisdom, strength, and ...

Narrator: But the king interrupted the Magi's speech ...

Herod: Yes, yes. Why are you here?

Narrator: The Magi continued,

Magi: Your Majesty, we have been traveling for a long time and our journey has brought us to you. We hope that you will be able to assist us.

Narrator: The king thought to himself,

Herod: Just what I thought. Beggars! More beggars.

Narrator: But the king said to the Magi,

Herod: Yes, many come to me for assistance, but few receive it.

Narrator: The Magi replied,

Magi: If you forgive me, you misunderstand, Your Majesty. We require no material thing from you. We have come for information.

Narrator: The king said,

Herod: Information? What kind of information?

Narrator: And the Magi answered,

Magi: Perhaps we should tell you how it is that we came to be here. Then you will understand, your Majesty.

Narrator: And Herod said,

Herod: Very well. But remember, as you say, I am a busy man.

Narrator: The Magi answered,

Magi: Of course, Your Majesty. As you know, we study the heavens. We have been advisors to many great rulers, such as yourself. And though we are here for information, we have also come to you with good news, Mighty King Herod. For we have seen something wondrous in the heavens. Have not your own advisors seen it?

Narrator: Herod impatiently shook his head, but the Magi were beginning to interest him. The Magi continued the story,

Magi: Yes, Your Majesty, there is a new star in the heavens. Brighter than them all. It is truly wondrous. We have never seen anything like it before.

Narrator: Herod began to wonder if they had not lost their minds. He had never had much confidence in stargazers. Too many of them in the past had simply told him what they thought he wanted to hear. But there was something different, something almost spiritual about these Magi that made him most uncomfortable. The Magi continued,

Magi: We know the stories of your people — the Jews — of the promise of a Messiah. We believe, Your Majesty, that this is his star! It is a sign to us — to you — to all your people — that he is to be born soon.

Narrator: The Magi then, hardly able to control their excitement,

Magi: Perhaps the king has been born already!

Narrator: In their excitement, the Magi had not noticed that Herod's face had grown pale. Only the chief servant, who stood beside them, took notice of it, and a cold shiver passed through him. He knew Herod, as did all the people of Jerusalem. Herod had grown murderous in his old age. Already he had killed one of his wives, his mother-in-law, an uncle, and three of his own sons! Caesar himself had said about Herod, "It is safer to be Herod's pig than his son!" And the chief servant had witnessed the murders of hundreds of others by order of the king. He remembered well the young high priest, Aristobulus, appointed high priest over the King's objections, for the young man was quite popular with the people. The king invited the young high priest to spend a short vacation at his summer palace in Jericho. One day, they went swimming in the pools there. The king, playfully, at first, began to dunk the young man under the water. And he continued until he was drowned. Of course, the king claimed it was an accident, but everyone knew the truth. But what could they do? He was king. Herod, having regained some composure, said,

> *Quality is all-pervading.*
> *And its use is inexhaustible.*
> *Fathomless.*
> *Like the fountainhead of all things.*

JE – The reason I'm asking this is because I want to be clear that what you mean by Quality in these terms. I'd like to try and keep clear what we mean specifically. ... I'm not a Christian myself, but I have an interest in Christianity. ... In Christianity, the metaphor of the virgin birth is where they use the metaphors of God as Jesus's Father, and Mary as 'Mother of God.' But alternatively, it also could be said possibly to mean that the real father of a baby is not the actual biological father, but the evolution that precedes...

HG – Yes, the Christian interpretation is that God mystically created the baby. This is the religious alternative to the idea that mystical Quality is the force acting within the real father and mother, creating the baby. Thus, when you're reading *ZMM*, you might interpret Pirsig as saying 'Quality' created the baby, Quality almost being a duplicate for the action of God. Materialists would say physical forces, operating throughout Darwinian evolution created the baby.

JE –What about the fact that murderer James Holmes was produced by evolution... so what would you say about that?

HG – I've been troubled by the notion of evil all my life and Pirsig in Zen says something like 'bad stuff happens'.... 'We don't like it, but it happens. This relates to one of the points in Pirsig's book *Lila*, which took me a long time to realize: In *Lila* the message is, I think, something like the following ... Evolution, for example, and lots of other circumstances, are dirty and slimy and smelly and a whole bunch of other negative things. But sometimes these are the very ugly narrow places that evolution, or even a human being, must go through to come out the other side and be 'better.' So, in outcome, this is a silver-lining thing, and this has been implicit in evolution all along. Some very tough, awful things have created positive outcomes, for example, what ended up being us. And that is a proper understanding of Dynamic Quality. We might not like it, but 'bad stuff happens, is here to stay, but sometimes is positive in outcome.

Now this guy Holmes: There is no way can I take him as a positive: he's an example of the awful, damnable things that human beings have had to suffer – Pirsig alludes to this in the final paragraph of *ZMM,* as we've seen. Unfortunately, looking at the bigger picture, we have to confront the fact that these things are just as much a part of the evolutionary process to make us who we are, as anything else. We may not appreciate it, we may not like it, we may think it's awful, but that's a fact that awful has been part of our biological evolutionary creation, and thus part of Quality.

Herod: What is it that you require of me, Magi?

Narrator: The Magi began to sense that perhaps Herod was not as happy as they about this news. But they proceeded anyway.

Magi: Your Majesty, we ask only that we be allowed to consult with your priests, so that we might know where this Prince is to be born. Surely you have sacred writings which they could consult?

Narrator: Herod said to the Magi,

Herod: This may take some time. I will have one of my servants take you to the dining chamber where you can rest and be refreshed with the hospitality of my house.

Narrator: Herod clapped his hands and another servant appeared and escorted the Magi from his presence. He needed time to think. When the Magi had left, the king gave his chief servant an icy stare and said to him,

Herod: You will inform the priests of this and that I will meet with them immediately.

Narrator: The chief servant bowed and Herod waved him from his presence. The chief servant, with some relief to be out of the king's presence, went to do as he was ordered. He wished he had sent the Magi away to begin with. But then he thought, if he had and the king found out about it and what they were seeking, then his life would have been worthless. It just may be anyway, for the king was getting old. He was unpredictable. No good could come of this, the servant thought ... and another cold shudder shook his body. The chief servant found the priests and quickly briefed them on the situation. One of the priests complained,

Priest: Not this Messiah nonsense again! We have no time to waste on such trivial matters. Doesn't the king realize that we are busy planning and conducting our temple rites and rituals? We have better things to do.

Narrator: But the chief servant replied,

Servant: We all have better things to do, but you were not there. You know how the king feels about such things. I saw it in his eyes — the anger, the madness. Heads may well roll in this matter and we had best take it seriously lest the heads are ours!

Narrator: Then the priests grew silent and pale, understanding the implications. But they would have to calm the king, assuring him that these rumors arose all the time among the people and never amounted to anything. They began to talk among themselves, ignoring the presence of the chief servant, who waited anxiously, ringing his hands. Suddenly, the door to the chamber burst open and in walked the king. The chief servant and the priests bowed and in unison said,

Servant and Priest: Your Majesty.

Narrator: The king said,

Herod: You have been informed of the situation?

Narrator: The priest replied,

Priest: Yes, Your Majesty.

Narrator: But the priests stood there as if frozen until the king roared,

Herod: Well?

Narrator: The chief priest, in a timid voice, said,

Priest: Your Majesty, we have heard all of this before. Rumor after rumor about a Messiah. And all of them proved to be groundless. You remember just last year, right here in the holy city, such a rumor was spread. But there was nothing to it. This, too, shall pass away.

Narrator: But Herod replied,

Herod: Yet never before have Magi showed up at my door, my very door, mind you, following a star and looking for the King of the Jews!

Narrator: Herod's face had turned blazing red. The priest, seeking to soothe the king, replied,

Priest: Pagans, Your Majesty. They're pagans. They follow pagan ways. They know nothing of our faith. They look to the stars. They are fools on a fool's errand. Send the fools on their merry, foolish way.

Narrator: Herod stared at the priest, his eyes aflame, and the priest realized that this would not be enough to satisfy the king, so he said,

Priest: Your Majesty, I have another suggestion. Let us play along with these fools. I am certain there is nothing to what they say, but just in case, why not assist them and tell them that if they do find this king, to come back to tell you so that you can also come and pay homage? Then you can act to remedy the situation.

Narrator: At first, the king was still angry. How dare anyone think there could ever be a greater king than he or that he would bow before another! But slowly a smile spread across his face. He liked this plan. It was subtle but effective. So he said,

Herod: So be it. But these troublesome Magi wish to know where this king is to be born. What should I tell them?

Narrator: The chief priest took down some of the scrolls and conferred with the other priests for a moment. Then he pointed to a passage and the others nodded in agreement. Then he read to Herod,

Priest: Here are the words of the Prophet Micah,

> Bethlehem in the land of Judah,
> you are by no means the least of the leading cities of Judah;
> for from you will come a leader
> who will guide my people Israel.

Narrator: The king turned and left as quickly as he had entered, uttering the name,

Herod: Bethlehem ... Bethlehem ...

Narrator: And he had the troubling thought that somehow that city was connected to King David and that the Messiah was to be born in the lineage of David. But he quickly dismissed such thoughts. Bethlehem was but an obscure village. Nothing of any significance could possible happen there. But even if it did, he would take care of it, just as he had every other threat to his rule. So Herod called the Magi back together for a secret meeting. And he asked them questions this time. He asked,

Herod: When did you first see this star?

Narrator: One of the Magi answered,

Magi: It has been over a year now, Your Majesty.

Narrator: The Magi thought that at last the king was interested in their journey. But they did not know that he was trying to gather information for his own sinister purposes. For in asking when they first saw the star, he was trying to get some idea of the age of this child. Such information might be useful later. So when Herod had extracted all the information he could from them, he sent the Magi on their way, telling them all that his priests had advised — to go to Bethlehem and seek diligently for the child, making certain to come back to him if they found the newborn king so he could worship him, too. Herod was well pleased with his plan.

The Magi immediately started for Bethlehem. But as they camped that night, the star appeared again before them and, with exceeding great joy, they rose and followed it until they came to Bethlehem. There they found the Child with Mary his mother, and knelt down and worshiped him, presenting him with gifts fit for a king. That very night, the Magi had a dream. In it an angel from God said to them,

Angel: Do not go back to Herod as he desired, for he seeks to destroy the Child.

Narrator: So they arose the next day and went back to their country by another road. The very same night Joseph, too, had a dream. The angel of the Lord appeared to him and said,

Angel: Joseph, arise and take the Child and Mary to Egypt, for Herod will soon seek his life. All of you will be out of danger there. I will tell you when it is safe for you to return home.

Narrator: So Joseph arose and did as the Lord had commanded him. When Herod realized that the Magi had slipped his grasp and that they had tricked him, he tore through his palace in a rage. He ordered the priests who had advised him to be brought before him. He then gave them a new appointment — in prison ministry (for they would spend the remainder of their lives in prison). Then he summoned the general of his army and ordered,

Herod: General, you will take an armed force and go to Bethlehem. There you will search for this so called "King," and to make sure that you find him, you will execute every male child from one year old and younger.

Narrator: The general saluted and was turning to leave, when Herod said,

Herod: No, General. I must make sure that this matter is taken care of. You will kill every male child in Bethlehem two years and younger.

Narrator: Herod knew that the Magi had been seeking this Child at least a year, so the Child would have to be at least one year old. But just in case, he would leave nothing to chance. He would destroy every two year old and younger. The general saluted the king and then left. That very night his soldiers entered every home in Bethlehem, and before the night was over, some thirty male children had been killed. This he reported to Herod the next morning.

For the next year, Herod daily grew weaker. He ate little and slept less, for his sleep was filled with dreams that none of his advisors could interpret or would dare interpret. For in his dreams all the voices of those he had killed, especially the children, tormented him. And then came the same vision — of a star shining down on a small infant in a manger — an infant who radiated a light even brighter than the star. Near the end of his life, Herod was taken to his summer palace in Jericho. But before he left Jerusalem, he gave this order to his general,

Herod: You will arrest the leading citizens of Jerusalem. Cast them in prison. And make a public announcement that they will be executed the moment news reaches here that I have died. For I know that no one will mourn my death, but when it comes, you will make sure that there is mourning in Jerusalem.

Narrator: It was a fitting last order for the evil king. And several days later, in April of 4 B.C., Herod died. But his last order was not carried out. And no one, not even his own family, shed one tear of sorrow for him. That same night, in Egypt, the angel of the Lord came again to Joseph in a dream and said,

Angel: Get up, Joseph, and take the Child and his mother, and go back to the land of Israel, for those who sought his life are dead.

Narrator: And so Joseph did. And after another dream, he took his family to Galilee, away from the son of Herod who now ruled in his father's place.

So, dear listeners, even before the Christ Child was born, there were those who wanted to destroy him. It was but a sign of things

JE – I think this is very interesting, if painful point and worth exploring further. I mean, I can't but agree with you. I mean, I don't really want to agree with you, because after all, without wanting for a moment to minimize the horrible suffering of the victims, of Holmes' victims, the mechanisms, the weapons, the tools, the guns he used to do what he did were actually made by organizations that were themselves the production of an evolutionary belief that human beings need to arm themselves ... to defend themselves.

As far as dealing with the problem of evil in terms of Pirsig's book, I mean you're right, he doesn't really have an answer to the problem of evil. He says it happens and we'd rather it didn't happen and, of course, the last paragraph of the book does refer to evil and bad things going wrong very clearly. And, I mean, as a writer myself, I see evil stemming from the fact that evolution produced organic beings called humans, who have a variety of appetites. And some of those appetites are ones that benefit the human community, such as the appetite for love, the appetite for wanting to help people in their lives, the appetite for wanting to work hard.

But some of those appetites do not benefit the human community and the justification for regarding them as evil, regarding the acts as evil is very, very clear because, after all, if everybody behaved as James Holmes behaved in that cinema, human life would become extinct because everyone would be dead. And in some ways, in as much as anything good can come out of such a dreadful event, it warms the heart that there was a mechanism in place, created by human beings as well, for putting him on trial and investigating what happened, and the mechanism, despite the ability of society to just summarily execute him and kill him, did not do that, but actually gave an ordered trial and gave a jury, a group of people, the opportunity to make a calm and ordered decision about what to do with him. And I suppose I find all this a clear manifestation of Quality in a certain way, but perhaps we're getting off the point a little bit, which is really your own: What Quality is, and how the perception of Quality has affected your life. I mean, am I right in assuming that until reading Pirsig's book you just thought of quality in terms of the everyday, commercial meaning 'something of a high standard?'

HG –Yes, quality of products & services, with a lower case q, was a dominate usage and understanding when I grew up….

But to get back to Holmes for a minute, we can assume, that in *his own mind*, he would have seen his acts of killing as a glorious big success. He has no feeling whatsoever for the people who he injured. Now Pirsig approaches this problem of evil, and part of his thoughts, that have to be said here, is that Holmes was a product of a distorted upbringing, bad ideas taught in a twisted distorted society, along with a distorted imbalance of the news media… that made him the way he was. And so the action of Quality here has to be that enough people are horrified by this distorted society, that they will take to come for him. This is not just a story of long ago. It is for us, too, for the Magi continue their journey. They have come to this place, this day. And they bear the same news, "A King is coming — the King of kings."

Herod, like the Grinch, tried to keep Christmas from coming. It came anyway, but not to Herod. You see, Christmas still cannot come to those who are only troubled by his coming, who fear he will interfere with their lives, their power, their plans; who cannot allow him to sit enthroned in their hearts as King.

Christmas came, but not to Herod's advisors and to all like them — indifferent, too busy with their lives that they ignore him, who never even bother to call his name during this season that is named after him. But Christmas still does come — to the wise ones, who, like the Magi, kneel on bended knee in adoration and worship; who present him with all their gifts, even their very lives.

Will Christmas come to your heart, to your home this year?

action and try to beat down on these very things that are causing such awful things. But of course to do this, you've got to go way back into the problems of warfare and the glorification of killing and so forth. In the Holmes case, he learned of this glorification. But let's hope there are enough horrified people who will get busy to do something about it.

I think that the concept of Quality helps us connect with the person that we really are: To understand how to learn, and how to be creative, and how best to proceed with a good life outcome. Now getting back to what you were asking me a minute ago, as to what was my own feeling about Quality and what I believe about Pirsig's Quality. I said my first interpretation of Pirsig is this: Quality is the Mystical Force that runs the universe, just like a scientist would say that the laws of physics are what run the universe. In my first interpretation, I mentioned *Mystical*, which I think is more Phaedrus' position, and not so much Pirsig's.

Now, here's my own <u>second</u> interpretation of how I am affected by Pirsig's book and his Quality. This, my <u>non</u>-mystical interpretation, is a bit more involved, and thus harder to understand, and a whole lot harder to get used to. My own second version proceeds from Pirsig's statement on constructivism:

> *Quality is the continuing stimulus which our environment puts upon us to create the world in which we live. All of it. Every last bit of it.*

Now, Dynamic Quality is Pirsig's name for what does the *creating* (constructing) in our mind, and ONLY in our own mind. And in a certain sense, Pirsig's name for that which *runs* our mind. In this view, 'The universe' (the ONLY universe we have) is what Dynamic Quality has constructed in our own minds, and since Dynamic Quality creates and runs our own mind, then Dynamic Quality creates and runs the universe, or at least the only universe we know of. In summary: Dynamic Quality creates the subjects and objects of this world, because it's created them, along with the whole universe, and human babies, in (and ONLY in) our own mind.

Effectively, it's the only world we've got, because it's all, and ONLY, in our own mind. So, that's my restricted second interpretation of Pirsig's Quality, and where I think it fits overall. ... However realistically, in this second interpretation, Quality can't actually 'run' the 'real out there' universe, because what 'runs the real universe', like 'reality', is at rock bottom, unknowable. But certainly, Quality runs our own mind, and our own mind creates the universe in our mind, and that's the sense, at which Quality runs the universe. A physical scientist, who accepts constructivism, might eventually come around to agreeing with this second interpretation. Owen Barfield effectively says the same thing =>

"... when we study long-term changes in [human] consciousness, we are studying changes the people here seemed so strange with such strange ways — how would we know who we could trust? But then came that morning I knocked over the water jar, and had to go back to the well, long after the sun was high. My fear made me stumble, and suddenly you were there, reaching out a hand to catch the jar before it fell, with that smile of yours that brought such a look to your face, a look like I was the one you'd been waiting for all morning.

Our ways were so different, but it didn't seem to matter so much. We learned to speak a few words of each other's language and our babies were the same age. Your father gave Joseph work. I will never forget that first Passover in this wild land. I tried to tell you about it, about what it meant to us, though I wasn't sure you understood. But then you appeared at the door, skin full of new wine and the haunch of a lamb in your hands. "My Passover gift to you, my sister," you said. It was then I knew I could make a life here, even in the midst of strangers.

It feels different to be going home — not like I thought it would. Oh, it will be good to see my mother, my sisters — who knows how many babies have come since we left? But this morning when I woke, I looked around as the golden light of morning came in the window and shone upon Jesus' dark curls, then moved on to the blanket you helped me weave with its dark brown wool threaded through with deep purple. Then the light touched the new comb Joseph brought home from the market last week and suddenly my throat hurt and it almost felt like I was going to cry.

Oh, I will miss you, Ahjah. You are friend of my spirit — we meet at a place where differences don't matter. But, of course, we must go. We belong there, and our families are there. That is where we should be raising our son. Besides, it's safe now that Herod's gone.

But, is it? Safe, I mean? Sometimes when I lie awake and cannot sleep, I think of all that has happened. Of how the angel came and told me this child was to be like no other, a holy child, the Son of God — of how in a dream, the angels told Joseph how to save us all — of how my heart broke when I heard of the killings of every male baby in Bethlehem all because of our own sweet boy.

But I must confess that sometimes I try to forget all that. Like any mother, I dote on my firstborn — precious little one, his giggle like your own Memnon's, his eyes bright when he gets into mischief, and, oh, he does get into mischief.

Sometimes I think if we could just stay here, maybe we could live out our lives like other people — put Joseph's dreams behind us, forget the star that shone in the sky; forget how the shepherds knelt there in the straw, forget about the three foreigners who came with their treasures and talk of stars and prophecies. Sometimes I don't want to go back to Nazareth — even though it's home, returning there troubles me. I wonder what waits for us there and it makes me afraid, the questions twisting in my heart like a knife.

When I was a child, my father used to tell me that if we did our best to be good, to follow the Torah, God would never let any harm come to us. But then my sister Rachel, a tiny girl sweet as honey — she grew sick, then sicker with each passing day. One morning when I awoke, I heard my mother weeping and knew without asking that Rachel was dead. How could that be if what my father said was true?

Father taught me not to ask foolish questions, but even now I am troubled with strange ideas. Life isn't at all what I thought it was when I was a girl. It seems there is heartache in store for all of us, whether we follow the laws or not. Perhaps the truth is that we cannot get through life without it. Perhaps faith isn't about believing the laws will save us, but believing that God is with us always, even when life itself feels like it will break our hearts, and God seems as far away as the emperor's city of Rome. But like my papa used to say, that is probably just a silly girl's foolish talk.

Can you imagine? I once thought Egypt was the end of the world. Then look what happened. I found a tiny house of my own, a sunny street where people speak with kindness and children play, and I found the love of a friend. And I will say to you, foolish or not, I do believe whatever happens, wherever we are called to go, God is ever with us — in a stable in Bethlehem, in a dusty village in Egypt, in all the years that lie ahead of us, no matter what they bring. I just wish I could learn not to worry.

Well, we have a long journey ahead of us. I'll never forget you, Ahjah. I'll never forget the life we found here, even in Egypt. Even when our hair is white and our skin like parchment, we can hold our grandbabies and know that somewhere in a far land there is a sister much like ourselves. When the new baby comes, I pray it will be the girl you've been longing for. Good-bye ... good-bye.

The Life
And Ministry
Of Jesus

Never Too Late

by Pamela J. Tinnin

Matthew 3:1-12

Notes

A young girl meets John the Baptist and faces the questions we all face. Will we truly repent and choose the way of Jesus? Is it ever too late?

When your years grow long, a thing of great mystery happens. In your dreams and memories, every day becomes like yesterday. That is the way of it when I think back long ago, back to the time of the crazy one. People said he lived in a cave down by the Jordan, but we heard tell that he traveled all over that region. He talked like a prophet of old. There were many who said he was possessed, that he was in the grip of a demon.

I was just a girl then — a pretty one, too, even if it is me who says it. Ah ... beauty comes and goes, but back then it seemed like I would be young forever. My sister Anna and I spent our days helping our mother, but we found enough time to go down to the well, to smile at the boys as they passed by, each of us waiting for that one who would come to our father to ask for us in marriage.

We knew husbands would not be easy to find. Our father was a fierce trader, known for driving a hard bargain. He was also wise and knew the Torah like a rabbi. The men of the village would seek him out for conversation over a cup of wine — debating this law or that one long into the night.

I remember the morning that it all began, Anna and I beating the rugs out against the east wall, the morning sun warm on our backs. Our mother was inside gathering up the laundry. I looked up the street, shading my eyes against the sun. Papa was coming. He had been to the rabbi's house to talk about the crazy one, the one they called John the Baptizer. I watched my papa make his way down the street. He carried his walking stick and his face looked troubled. When Anwar, the sandalmaker, called out to him, he didn't even look up. He walked past us without saying anything and went inside. We could hear his voice, my mother's soft answer, but we could not make out the words.

My mother came out and told us to bring the rugs inside, that we were going on a journey. The rabbi had chosen my father to go to the camp of the Baptizer. The rabbi had dreamed that this son of Zechariah and Elizabeth would bring word of the Messiah — that somehow, crazy or not, God would speak through him. Of course, the rabbi could not go — the elders would think he had lost his own mind. But he trusted my father to see the truth — or the lie of it. And Papa wanted us to see for ourselves.

It would be a day and a half walking, so we packed up bread and dried fish, the last of the dates, and a few figs. My father took two skins and filled them with water, and slung them over his shoulder. We carried blankets and wore our winter cloaks. The days had grown colder, and we could hear the wind crying in the leaves.

We walked all that day, stopping only when the sun was at its highest for a bite to eat. My feet grew sore as we set out again, but Papa would not let us stop, not until it was almost dark. Just at dusk we saw the flames of a fire against a small hill. My father stopped us and called out, his hand on the handle of the knife he had hidden in his belt, "I am Martin, merchant from the village of Mizrah, with my wife and daughters."

A voice came back from beyond the fire. "I am Simeon, son of old Simeon. My brother Asher travels with me, going home to Naphtal. You are welcome to share our camp." We were glad for the company and opened our bags and spread our food on a kidskin. The two strangers — not much more than boys — offered dried olives, bitter and salty, and some cakes that had grown hard and a little musty, but still tasted of spice.

As we ate, we listened to the brothers speak of how they had taken a flock of sheep to sell in Jerusalem, and of the wonders of the city. They told of the market where a poor man could buy a ragged dove for sacrificing, or a rich man a slave to do his bidding. They said beggars and magicians and acrobats crowded around, yelling for attention; that there was a man who swallowed flames and another who could pull gold coins from your hair. Anna and I laughed at the thought of it.

The hour grew late and we went off to our beds. I remember looking up at the stars and wondering how such things could be. The last thing I heard was the sizzle of burning pitch, and my mother's high, sweet voice singing an old song.

We women slept until the sun woke us. We were not far from the Jordan. Simeon told us that he and Asher would go with us. They wanted to see what went on when the Baptizer preached.

The land was nothing but sand and dry grass, rocky hills with a few withered trees. Ahead we could see the dusty green of the bushes along the river. As we made our way down to the shore, I remember we could hear something in the distance. At first, I thought it was nothing but the hum of locusts, but when we got closer, I could tell it was the voice of a man, and the sound of people singing and chanting.

When we got nearer, we saw many gathered there. There were tents and little huts; you could smell the smoke of the cooking fires. Some people went on about their work, women cooking, men gathering up thin sticks of wood, children running and playing. Hundreds stood near the edge of the river, some up to their ankles in the brown water. Some on the shore danced; others fell to their knees offering prayers to the heavens; but mostly people watched the man who stood farther out, the waves rippling around his middle, his hands raised to the sky. He was not old, but as withered as the trees, thin and browned by the sun, his hair a tangled mass around his face.

"Repent in the name of the Lord," he cried, over and over. "Make your ways straight." I saw a boy younger than me step into the water and stumble toward him. The Baptizer spoke words we could not hear, and then pushed the boy backward into the water, calling out the words of a prayer. First one, and then another came, rushing out of the muddy swirl, choking and gasping, but praising God and crying out their thanks.

He turned in our direction, and I could hear his raspy whisper above all the other voices. "Do not wait," he said, "Now is the time to choose, to prepare yourself. I baptize you with water, but there is one who will come after me who will baptize you with fire." Then he raised his finger, pointed, and spoke again. "But do not choose lightly — for if you choose to follow him, you must change your life." Perhaps it was just the sun shining off the water, but when he looked up, there was such light in his face. I knew then he spoke the truth, that the one he proclaimed was the Messiah.

I wish I had listened that day. I wish I had stepped into the water and felt his heavy hands on my head, pushing me under. I wish I had spread my blankets there on the banks of the Jordan and waited for the one who was to come.

But in that moment when I moved toward the water, my papa's voice rang out, echoing all along the river, just one word, over and over, "Blasphemy ... blasphemy...." We left then, and the brothers with us. We walked away from the river, across the wilderness, and back to our lives. Anna and I did not know it yet, but we had found our husbands. Not long after, on a Sabbath afternoon, Simeon and Asher came with their father and an agreement was made. Before my next birthday my sister and I were brides. We went to live in Naphtal, neighbors and a comfort to each other all our days.

Through all the years, we lived by the rules, followed the rabbis; we paid our tithes, made sacrifices on the holy days. We did well — look around you. But some nights when I cannot sleep I feel an ache — an emptiness that nothing seems to fill; a feeling that all this wealth and comfort stand for nothing. Certainly it did not protect us — the plague that took our parents; Anna, a widow most of her days; me with three babies dead before one lived, and of the two who survived, the youngest gone to fight with the rebels and lost to me as surely as if he, too, were dead.

John the Baptist told of a different way to live, a way of living for others, a way where death would not matter. He said that the one who came after him would teach us. But I was afraid. One time I heard the man Jesus was preaching in the next village — I stayed home and kept the shutters locked. No use asking for trouble.

Oh ... I haven't been a bad person. I give alms to the beggars who pull at my cloak; I have never been cruel. But each of us knows in our hearts what kind of life we have lived ... me most of all, an old woman whose years are as worn down as a candle on its last burning.

There are some who say Jesus will come again. That it could be any day, this very night. There are some who say we will find him if we keep looking. That there is nothing beyond his forgiving. But I cannot put that day out of my mind — the air filled with a hundred voices singing and praying, a man waist deep in dirty water, telling me to choose. I remember wanting to speak, to step into the river — and all I did was walk away — just walk away.

Do you ever wish you could turn back the years? That you could do it all over? Do you ever wish you could go back and find the courage to change things? But we cannot begin again ... can we? Can we?

My Name Is Levi

by Peter K. Perry

Mark 2:13-17

Notes
The tax collector Levi, who becomes Matthew, tells his story.

My name is Levi, son of Alphaeus. I am not important in the way the world judges importance. But I am important in the eyes of God, and in the end, that's really all that matters. Let me tell you how I learned this lesson ... perhaps you will see yourself in my story.

As I said, I am Levi, son of Alphaeus. I grew up in the village of Nahum, what is called today Capernaum. Capernaum is a beautiful village built on the northwestern shore of the Sea of Galilee. It is a fishing village, of course, but the area is also very fertile, producing abundant crops of grapes and olives and barley. On the hills far outside of the city, shepherds tended their herds of sheep and goats. But Capernaum is also a popular stopping off place for the traders who journey from Damascus to Samaria and Jerusalem and the cities on the coast of the Great Sea.

My father was not a fisherman, or a farmer, or a shepherd ... he was an innkeeper. And so our livelihood came not from the water or the land, but from the flow of travelers. As a boy I would watch them as they enjoyed a day of respite from their journeys. They enjoyed the meals my mother prepared. My father tended to the needs of our guests and served the meals. I took care of the guests' animals, feeding and watering the donkeys and the camels, and guarding the packs which they bore.

I remember one morning I was fetching a guest's donkey from the stable. The donkey was being cantankerous, and I pulled on the harness, but the beast wouldn't budge. I got behind it and carefully tried pushing it. Nothing. I screamed at it; I tried to bribe it with a carrot. Nothing I did could get that donkey to move. Then the owner came out of the inn. He laughed. "Old Ezekiel won't budge, son," he said. "At least not for you. But watch this!" The man looked the donkey in the eye and he said, "Ezekiel, follow me." That donkey sprang to its feet and promptly fell in line behind the man as he started down the lane out of town. I ran to catch up.

"How did you do that, sir?" I asked. "I tried and tried, and I couldn't get that old donkey to move an inch!"

"Son," he said, "Ezekiel trusts me. He knows I will take good care of him. When he hears my voice, he will follow me anywhere."

It wasn't too long after that when the trouble all started. My mother grew sick and died. My father tried to keep the inn open, but it was hard without mother's help. Fewer and fewer guests came to stay with us.

Finally, I had to look for work. I was apprenticed out to a man who worked for the Roman government, collecting taxes. Apprentice! Now there's a funny word ... slave is more like it! I did what I was told, even when what I was told to do was dishonest. I manned the tollbooth outside of Capernaum, where the road nears the sea. I was told to collect the Roman duties plus twenty percent. My master kept ten percent of the overage, and the soldiers who were stationed just beyond the tollbooth got the other ten percent. I got nothing but a subsistence wage and the undying hatred of everyone who had to use the roadway. People shunned me, even the people my age with whom I had grown up. I was the tax collector, though I never received a penny of the ill-gotten gains. Even my father was ashamed of me.

For three years I served my master in this way. And then one day, the soldiers demanded fifteen percent instead of ten percent. My master objected and refused to increase the amount the soldiers received. The next morning he was found floating face down in the Sea of Galilee. The soldiers came to me that morning and demanded fifteen percent. I agreed, and I kept the extra five percent for myself. I decided that since everyone already thought so poorly of me, I might as well be the man they thought me to be. I became the master I had always hated.

But though I now had money, I was never happy. I trusted no one. No one trusted me. I believed in nothing. No one believed in me. I just did my job, watched my back, and dreamed of the days long ago, before my mother had died, before father had lost the inn, when life had been worth living. Literally, at night I dreamed of my childhood. It was the only time I had ever been happy.

For a while I thought the money would make things all right again. I became wealthy. I bought a house, new clothes, and made investments. I even gave money to the synagogue, though the rabbi acted as though he didn't want it from me. I was still shunned. I was still despised.

One of my old friends came to talk to me one day. He said, "Levi, why don't you give up this work you do for the Romans? You don't need it anymore. You could do anything you want. Why don't you just quit?"

I scoffed at him. "Do you think people would just forget my past? Do you think all would be forgiven? I don't. No, Joshua, no. I am like a leper. People are afraid of me. People love to hate me. No. I cannot change." But Joshua's words weighed heavy on my mind. Deep down inside, I wanted to change. I just didn't believe I could. I didn't know where to start.

The next morning I took my usual place in the tollbooth by the sea. It was usually pretty quiet in the morning, but this morning was different. A preacher was teaching a crowd not too far away. Sometimes when the wind was right, I could hear his words. I strained to listen. He spoke words of hope to the people around him. He told them that God loved them. He told them that God believed in them. He told them that God would bless them, even though they were poor and powerless, even though they were hungry and thirsty, even though they mourned, even though they were persecuted, even though they were sinners. Strange words from this strange man. He spoke of being made new, of being reborn, of having the Spirit of God within us. He said that God makes all things new. He had been speaking a long time when someone offered him a drink from an old wine skin. He held it up and he said to the crowd, "Do you put new wine in old wineskins like this?"

Everyone laughed. "Of course not," he said, "for when the new wine ferments, it bubbles up with excitement and it bursts the old wineskin. You must put new wine in new wineskins." I swear as he said those words, he looked at me. I looked away, but I heard him say, "So it is with our lives. If we want to be different inside, we must be different outside as well. If we would change our hearts, we must change our lives."

He taught some more, but I was too busy thinking to listen. Could he have been talking to me? Could the teacher by the sea have known how much I wanted to change? Could he know how much I longed to be the person I knew I could be, the person I believed God wanted me to be? I had been a tax collector for a long time. I had cheated my brothers for a long time. I had served the Romans for a long time. I had nurtured my own self-loathing for a long time. I wasn't sure that I could change.

When I looked up, he was standing right in front of me. And he said, "Levi, follow me."

And I did. I followed him. I learned from him. And I never, ever went back to the tollbooth. Oh, it took some time for the people to understand that I could change. The religious people especially, it seems, had a hard time believing that I could change. The scribes and the Pharisees ... I remember ... before Jesus left Capernaum, he and the disciples ate a meal at my house. I was so happy that night. But the Pharisees and the scribes complained, saying, "How can he eat with this tax collector and all of these other sinners?" It hurt, but Jesus caught my eye, and he said to the scribes and the Pharisees, "Those who are well have no need of a physician, but those who are sick; I have come to call not the righteous but sinners." Jesus was my physician. He healed a hurt deep inside that most people didn't even know was there. To most people, I was just the tax collector. I was a sinner. Even I saw little more than what they saw. But Jesus saw what no one else saw. Jesus saw a child of God, a soul loved by God.

That night, when I finally fell asleep despite my excitement, I dreamed again of my childhood. I dreamed of the day when the old donkey Ezekiel wouldn't move. I dreamed of the old traveling merchant and the way he said, "Ezekiel trusts me. He knows I will take good care of him. He will follow me anywhere." When I awoke from the dream, I realized that I had been much like that donkey, except that I trusted no one and followed no one.

Now when people ask me why I followed Jesus that day ... why I just left everything behind and followed him, I just tell them about the old donkey named Ezekiel. I don't really know why I followed Jesus. I know that I was tired of being a stubborn, angry, foolish sinner. My heart was ready for a change. When Jesus said, "Levi, follow me," I at long last heard a voice that I knew I could trust, and so I followed. I hope and pray that others will hear the voice and will follow, too. For this is not just my story. It is our story. God makes us all new.

Living Water

by Pamela J. Tinnin

John 4:7-30

Notes
A woman tells of the struggles and trials of her life and of how a seemingly chance encounter with a man at a well brings new life and salvation.

It was a day like any other. To the east the sky was just beginning to streak with light when Enoch and I rose. I busied myself getting food for him, yesterday's bread, a bit of dried fish, the last of the grapes, withered and tough. His temper is not the best when he first rises, and oh, he was in a mood that day. Couldn't find his sandals — tore the bedding apart looking, his voice loud, using words that made me glad the priests weren't there to hear.

Enoch's not a bad man — certainly no worse than any other. I can't complain — I don't go hungry; I'm not sleeping on the streets. Besides, you know what they say — a bird in the hand....

After he left for the weaver's shop, I put things in order, swept out the corners, even mended Enoch's good robe. I had propped the shutters open, but there was no breeze and the heat rolled into the room. Such a dry year — the hills brown without a blade of grass; the goats and sheep stand weak and thin, their heads hanging low.

When the sun was at its highest, I put on my veil, picked up the heavy water jar, and, balancing it on my hip, started out for the well. Each day I waited until there was no chance of meeting anyone — I could not stand the other women with their pointing and whispering, the way they kept me back from the well until they had all filled their jars.

It was so hot. As I walked past the house of Philomel and her mother, I saw the curtain pulled aside and the gleam of dark eyes.

By the time the well was in sight, my lips felt cracked, and my throat ached for water. Then I saw him there, a man sitting by the well. I almost turned around and started back, but I could not. There wasn't a drop of water in the house and what was I to do? As soon as he sees I am a Samaritan, I thought, he won't bother me.

I stepped up next to the well and he looked up at me. I could see he was a young man, his face lined and dark from the sun, his hair dusty and tangled. I jumped when he spoke. "Give me a drink," he said. "You are a Jew," I said, "and I am a Samaritan — and yet you ask me for a drink? Why, what could you use to drink? I only have one jar." Everyone knows a Jew wouldn't let his lips touch anything a Samaritan had touched.

Reaching for the jar, he said something that made no sense. "If you only knew what God gives and who it is that is asking you for a drink, you would ask him, and he would give you life-giving water." He tipped the jar and drank and drank, then wiped his mouth, smearing the dust. Life-giving water? What was all this? Some tale he'd thought up — everyone knows that the prophet Jacob had given us this well — who was this to claim he was greater than Jacob? He spoke again, and told me that whoever drinks water from this well would be thirsty again, but whoever would drink the water he offered would never thirst.

I laughed at that, and let him know I wasn't taken in that easily. "Well, then give me that water — then I would never have to come to the well again."

"Go and get your husband and come back."

I looked away, and stepped back. But he was looking and waiting. I could hardly speak above a whisper. "I have no husband."

I looked at the ground, thinking of all that people said of me, "Why she's no better than a prostitute ... She'd sell herself for a bed and a bit of food ..." But when the man spoke his voice was kind, "No, he is not your husband, though you have been married five times before." And then he told me all about my life.... He knew everything about me ... everything.

I had such dreams when I was a girl. You may not believe it, but I was pretty then. People would stop to admire my curls, my plump cheeks, my long eyelashes. As I approached the age of marriage, there were lots of village boys who found one excuse or another to pass by our street. Of course, my father had no intention of choosing some hairless youth with no money and few prospects. No, for me he wanted only the best. That's how I came to the house of Menachem. He and my father had been boys together. He had been alone since the year before, when his wife was taken by the fever that strikes in times like these, when the heat seems like it will go on forever, the water is low in the wells, and even the oases seem dry and brown.

At first I was happy. Menachem spoiled me — always buying me little gifts and sweetmeats, speaking kindly to me, and quick with a compliment. My friends envied me and I must confess I flaunted my new-found fortune — the purple cloth he brought me on a buying trip in the north, the feasts I served the friends, the silver bracelets that twined around my wrist.

My parents were pleased to see me settled in such comfort, to know they had no worries for their last days. None of us saw the truth, at least not then. As the first year passed, my husband changed, or maybe it was just his old ways returning. Every night he would pour wine until he emptied the jar, then call me to bring another, until his voice grew loud and his steps grew unsteady. So many times he fell into sleep at the meal, his head forward on his chest, the room filled with the sound of his snoring.

Thanks be, he was never cruel — but soon there were mornings when he wouldn't go in to market until almost midday, and business began to suffer. He left more and more up to Ben-Adam, his manager. Then came the trip to Egypt to buy goods. I stayed behind, me four months with child. Week after week passed, then a month, but I didn't expect him back until just before the harvest festival. Early one morning I was beating the rugs outside against the front wall, sneezing as dust billowed around me, when I saw Ben-Adam, his face clouded with heavy thoughts, a weary looking man hobbling along with him. I remember stepping back, trying to keep them from telling me the news they had brought, the news I could see on their faces. There wasn't much to tell — harsh words said at a wineshop, the flash of a skinning knife, my husband's blood staining his beard, and in the sixteenth summer of my life I was a widow.

But that wasn't the end of it — by sundown that same day I learned Menachem had mortgaged everything to the moneylenders. They told me that out of kindness they would give me until the end of the week to find another place. Where was I to go except back to my own village, to my parents, and them with four young ones still at home? The day I was packing, Ben-Adam came. A shy and awkward man, he could barely speak the words. A widower himself, he would take me to wife if I would have him. He had been wise with his earnings and had enough to open a small shop. An old man even then, his hair and beard were white, only three teeth rested in his mouth, and his eyes clouded with age. It was a kind offer, but I was just a girl. All I could think of were days and nights with this one who held my arm with his bony hand. Then the child moved within me, and I knew I had little choice. How could I know I would lose the baby before it came to term ... and Ben-Adam would be dead, too, before the year was out.

The third time I married, it was for love, a young and handsome man with an easy laugh. He sang with a voice that brought tears to the hardest eyes. We never had much money, and no babies came, but we were happy. Our third winter together, in the coldest month when ice crusted the water jar, a plague came to our village. He sickened and died and I was alone once more. One after another, my husbands died. The years passed. I wasn't so pretty any more and the stories spread from village to village that I brought ill fortune to any man who came near. I guess Enoch was desperate enough or lonely enough that he didn't care — or maybe that's why he never married me.

I kept thinking I'd found the answer — wealth and comfort; a fine husband; my own shop. I had such dreams and they all came to nothing. Finally life was just day-by-day doing what I had to do to get by. With each day that passed, my heart withered within me, as parched as the land itself.

I see people who have riches, fine homes, and cattle. I see those who fall in love and live to grow old together. I see women who bear healthy babies to fill their lives with laughter and the silly games of childhood. Those same people sneer at me as I pass. Once I was filled with envy for their easy lives, but no more. I know too well that life is never what it seems. I see how frightened they are that someone will steal what they have; how worried they become that love will grow cold; I see how children sometimes turn against their parents, and abandon them to live out their days alone. I see how quickly a fever can turn to death and leave your life in pieces. I am nothing but a Samaritan woman with little knowledge and certainly no special gift of wisdom, but is not the truth of it that we all live with broken dreams? And nothing — not gold or beauty or power — can keep us from the pain of life or heal the broken places.

At first I tried to forget the stranger at the well. But I could not forget how he knew me ... how his words spoken in the heat of the day washed over me like a cool stream ... how he understood the deepest secrets of my heart.... He is no ordinary man ... he is the Christ. And he found me. He came to me, as poor a creature as I am ... and he comes to you.... He comes bringing life-giving water, the living water of God's love. All we must do is offer him our lives — all the dried up, empty places — and we will be refreshed, renewed, and filled.

Kneeling Before Him

by Pamela J. Tinnin

Luke 10:38-42

Notes

A neighbor woman and good friend of Mary and Martha tells how each chose their own way to honor Jesus.

Not one word about Mary — I won't hear it. She is as dear to me as a sister; we were in and out of each other's houses from our first steps. Oh, I know she spent a year's wages on nard and then used it all on the Nazarene's feet. I was there — I heard the gasp of the elders when she removed her veil, uncoiled her hair, hair that gleamed like copper in the flickering light of the oil lamps, heavy hair like streaks of fire that fell down her back almost to the floor. If there be fault in Mary, it may be that she's always been a bit vain about her hair — but then, what did she do but kneel before him and taking her hair, wipe his feet with it — think of it. Wiped his feet with her beautiful hair.

Martha was white with embarrassment when she turned from making supper, her fingers sticky with dates, to see her sister there on the floor. Martha tries so hard to temper Mary's flightiness, but she's always rushing off, doing something that raises the neighbors' eyebrows, starts them whispering. Uncovering her hair, and touching a man's feet ... and certainly no kin to their family, and from all accounts, a troublemaker.

That's when the sharp-faced man sneered and spoke loud enough for all to hear, the man whose eyes are always looking this way and that, like an animal backed into a corner. They call him Judas. Some say he's a thief, and maybe worse, but I'm not one to gossip. His words were hard, accusing Mary of waste, of taking from the poor. But the man, Jesus, said the strangest thing: "Leave her alone. She bought it so that she might keep it for the day of my burial. You always have the poor with you, but you do not always have me."

She loves him — that's obvious. At first I thought it was the love for a husband, but watching her that night, it's not like that at all. Many follow him these days, listening to his teaching; a few even whisper he's the Messiah. With her, it's different, I think — after all, he brought her brother back from the dead. When Mary looked up at him there was something in her eyes, like I've seen only once, on the face of an old holy man who was looking to the heavens, his hands raised in prayer.

There is talk that the priests want to rid themselves of him. They think he's dangerous. Old Hannah told me that the fortune-teller in the square, the one with the withered arm, has foretold the Nazarene's death, that he'll never leave Jerusalem alive — but then that one says many things that never come to pass.

No, matter, I won't listen to bad talk about Mary. When I lost baby Ethan last year, she was the one who stayed with me; she fed me spoonful by spoonful; she bought balm and rubbed it on my temples; she even sang for me when I couldn't sleep. Truth be told, she kept me from going mad.

I loved him so, my firstborn.... If I'd known I'd only have him for so short a time, not even two years, I would have held each moment like a rare jewel. I would have marked each day by putting to memory each precious thing. The day he smiled and I saw the white of a tooth. The way his hair curled with sweat when he slept in the heat of the day. His giggle when I scooped river water over his head and it ran down his fat little arms. My mother and the other old women tell me I'm young, I can have another ... but I would give any amount to have just one more day with him, 300 denarii, 600 ... anything.

Life goes by day by day, and the hours are filled with the sameness of things. Each day I'd rise in the morning, eat the last night's leftover bread and a fig, sweep out our room, beat the rugs against the wall, go to the well and return with the heavy water jar on one hip, the baby on the other. How could I know how quickly it could all change? I didn't see that in one moment, in the time it takes for one breath, what you love most can be torn from you, leaving your arms and your heart empty.

If we knew that, if we could keep it in our minds every morning when we wake, remind ourselves of it each night when we lay down to sleep, would we live our lives differently? Would we always speak with kindness? Would we sit outside together in the evening and watch the disappearing sun fill the sky with colors? Would we kiss our babies more? I don't know — I'm just a peasant girl with no learning, and certainly small wisdom.

Maybe if I'd been a better mother, a better wife ... maybe if we'd sacrificed a calf instead of that tiny goat kid ... maybe the baby would be sleeping now in the basket that still sits in the corner. Even yet, there is a weight pressing my heart into stone.

But this Jesus ... he says it doesn't have to be that way. Jesus says that love is stronger than death. That we will never be parted from the ones we love. He says that God loves us and cares for us, suffers with us when we think we cannot take one more thing, gives life where there is death. Mary told me that all those laws the priests quote again and again aren't nearly as important as trying to live every day with love. Have you ever heard of such a thing? Just to love. Jesus says God doesn't want sacrifices — goat kids or lambs. All God wants is our hearts.

I don't understand it all — I lay awake late last night, the light from the stars shining through the shutters, and I thought about everything that's happened. What he teaches is so different from what the priests at the temple say. Mary plans to follow him to Jerusalem; she's going to walk with him when he enters the gates. And, oh, it will be grand, she says. Some say he's going to declare himself a king. Some say he'll throw the Romans out of all Judea. There is much talk of rebellion.

But the other night in Bethany, there was no talk of kings, or battles, or conquering the world. He came in, some of his disciples, too, and just sat there, stretching his dusty feet out before him. I could tell he was tired, the skin shadowed under his eyes, the way he slumped on the stool. Mary came in and went right to him. Kneeling, she undid his sandals, and placed them to the side. Then the rich fragrance of nard filled the room.

I watched Mary rub the soreness from his feet, Martha clucking her tongue about the waste. Slowly Mary untwined the thick braid — her hair must have felt like fine silk against his calloused skin. He reached out and touched her shoulder, mumbling his thanks, and something else, too, so soft I couldn't make out the words, something about peace. Then Mary closed her eyes and bowed her head. For a moment, I thought she was weeping. It was still in the room, and felt so strange, like we were in a great temple, with God right there with us.

Then there was the sound of laughter from the street. Mary stood, and went to help Martha, and we all went back to what we were doing.

My husband Elias is angry, threatening to beat me, though he never would. He tells me this is no business for a good Jew, much less a woman, to get all worked up about — that I should stop asking questions and let things lie. Elias is older, and he knows best. He says that this man from Nazareth is just one more trickster like all the others who perform magic for money. That all this talk of love is foolish, nothing more than looking for an easy way. Disobeying the laws will only lead to trouble, he says, and I suppose he's right.

But, Jesus' words ... I can't get them out of my mind.

Well, I have to work to do — can't be wasting all day here by the well.

You know, Elias is wrong about one thing. Love is never easy. Sometimes it costs everything ... everything. And the man from Nazareth knows it — I can tell by the sadness in his eyes.

The sky's getting dark; I'd better get home before it rains.

Holy Week
And
Easter

Just A Jar Of Water

by Peter K. Perry

Luke 22:7-13

Notes

A Maundy Thursday story from the man in whose house Jesus and his disciples celebrated the Passover in the Upper Room.

I remember the days of that week. They were busy days for me anyway, but they were made much busier because of the festival. The city was a madhouse. Some were saying that over a million-and-a-half pilgrims had come to Jerusalem that year. Nearly 200,000 lambs were needed for the Passover meals which would be celebrated. On the day of Unleavened Bread, the smell of toasting flour filled the streets. Every home had been rented out for the Passover celebrations. It was madness, and it made me wish that we had moved away from the city when Father died.

I don't know why we stayed on in Jerusalem. We could have left. We could have gone home to be with my mother's brothers. Life would certainly have been much easier for us there. But we stayed. I guess leaving our home so soon after he died would have been just one more sorrow in our lives. We needed the familiarity of our little home. We needed the reminders of life the way it had once been — reminders of days when Mother and Father would fill our home with neighbors and friends for celebrations and festivals. For a while after Father died, those friends and neighbors would look in on us every day. But after a time, the friends stopped coming, and the neighbors only came by rarely.

Father had been a trader of linens. He was good at what he did but not so good that he left us with any money. Mother had been sick for several years before Father died. Father always said she would be the first to die, but he was wrong. And so, when he died, I was the only one left to care for her. We had a place to live, and some of the folks who had done business with Father continued to do business with me, despite my youth and inexperience. I was only fifteen years old, but I ran Father's business as best as I could, and I took care of my mother.

Please don't misunderstand what I'm about to say, for I love my mother. But I was getting tired of all I had to do for her. She rarely left our house. She wasn't strong enough to prepare the meals or wash the clothes. So I did those things for her. People would say to me, "John, you ought to get a wife." I always smiled and said, "Yes, I should. I think I will go down to the marketplace and pick one out — right after I finish changing mother's bed, delivering this order of linens, fixing dinner, paying my taxes, and honoring the Sabbath the way the rabbis say I should!"

I knew the proverb by heart, for it had been quoted to me so often! "A wife of noble character who can find? She is worth far more than rubies...." You know, truthfully, getting married would have been nice, and I was certain I would eventually find the right woman with whom I could share my life. I just hadn't met her yet. Maybe I was being forced to grow up too fast, but all of the young women my age seemed so childish! I used to hear them prattle on and on about babies and bat mitzvahs and what young man was in love with what young woman! I heard them everyday ... when I went to the well to draw water.

I guess that was the worst part of my life. I didn't really mind most of what I had to do to keep our lives together, for after all I loved my mother. But there was one thing I really hated. I hated carrying the water. The girls at the well seemed respectful of me, but I knew they were just feeling sorry for me. Most of the people who saw me carrying my water jar every day knew of our situation — knew I only did these things that no self-respecting man would do because I had no choice. We couldn't afford to hire someone to do the woman's work at our house. And mother couldn't do it. So I did. I didn't like the fact that people felt sorry for me, pitied me, but I could handle it.

Far worse than the pity of my countrymen were the taunts of the Romans in the city. They missed no opportunity to antagonize a Jew. I was the object of their ridicule. More than once they questioned my manhood. More than once they knocked the jar from my hands for sport. "In Rome," they said, "only slaves and women carry water! Which are you? You're not a slave, are you? Then you must be a woman!"

A man carrying a jar of water ... what a spectacle, what a sight to see! I hope they enjoyed their laughing, for I certainly did not. I was hurting inside as I longed for something more in my life, and that jar of water had become for me a symbol of all the hurt I had known, and all of the dreams I had long since abandoned. That jar carried more than water — it carried my shame, my grief, my loneliness. A man carrying a jar of water!

On the day of Unleavened Bread, I rose early as I did every day. I had not slept well. I had dreamed that our home was filled with people for the Passover Seder, and I was busy serving them. What foolishness! As though I had time to care for strangers on top of everything else! In the dream, there was a man at the head of the table. He had around him many followers who seemed to worship him and fear him and love him, all at the same time. They were laughing and telling stories and enjoying the meal. But then the man at the head of the table said something that upset them. Some grew angry, others were crying, and still others just looked bewildered. I moved among them filling their cups with wine, bringing them bread to eat. It was a curious dream indeed. Who knows where such dreams come from, from what wild imaginings, from what divine prompting?

I looked in on mother before beginning the daily chores. She was still sleeping, so I went about my work. When I began to prepare breakfast, I heard mother stirring. She called out my name, and I went in to her. "John," she said, "I had a most curious dream. I dreamt of the Passover. I dreamt that our home was filled with people as it used to be before your father died. I dreamt that we celebrated the Seder in our Upper Room."

"Mother," I said, "isn't that funny, for I had a similar dream."

"John," she said to me, "it would be so nice to see our house full of people again. I miss it so." And there was a look of quiet resignation in her eyes as she remembered the way things used to be.

The look in her eyes filled my mind as I went the well that morning to bring the water. It would be nice to celebrate the Passover again. It would be nice to hear laughter in our house once more.

Such were my thoughts as I made my way back through the crowded streets with my jar of water. The streets were filled with pilgrims. Passover was a happy time for them, as they remembered the story of our people's liberation from bondage in Egypt. How mightily God had acted! How wondrously he turned our sadness to joy! How swiftly he set us free from our oppressors! Not even the Roman presence in the city could dampen the spirit of the season for those who had traveled far to celebrate at the temple. But I did not share the pilgrims' joy. All I felt was the weight of my life, like the weight of the jar of water I carried every day.

"Hey, you, with the water!"

Oh, no, I thought to myself, another Roman pig making fun of me. I turned, but it was a not a Roman who had called out to me. The man who had called to me, and his friend, were Jews. They looked familiar, but I wasn't sure where I had seen them before. "Yes," I said.

"Shalom. This may seem odd, friend, but do you know a place where we may celebrate the Passover?"

And suddenly it dawned on me that I knew these men ... from my dream. They had been in my house, in my dream. I shivered, unsure of what this all meant.

"Follow me," I said, quietly and uncertainly.

I took them home and invited them in. "Our master told us to follow you to a home and to ask the master of the house if we might use a room for the Passover."

"I know I am young, but I'm the master of the house. It is just me and my mother. I ... we ... hadn't planned on having guests, for we are poor and she is sick. I have much work to do. I cannot prepare a Passover meal."

"We will prepare it for you, and you will be our guests, if we may use your home."

"Who's there?" called my mother.

"Some men who want to celebrate the Passover in our home," I answered. And turning to the men, I heard myself saying, "Yes ... yes, tell your master that you may observe the Passover here. We have a large room upstairs that you may use. Let me show you ..."

I took them upstairs, and they immediately set about preparing, but I stopped them, and I asked, "How is it that you asked me? Out of all the people in the streets today, how is it that you asked *me* about a place for the Passover?"

"Our master, Jesus of Nazareth, told us to look for a man carrying a jar of water. You were the only one we saw."

That night, they came. I had heard of Jesus, of course. Who in Jerusalem hadn't? And though I was busy, I was curious, and I took time to share in the work, and to celebrate the Passover with Jesus and his followers. Mother even found new strength, came out of her room, and climbed the stairs to join in the meal. I listened as the man, Jesus, spoke. Something in his words, something about who he was, drew me to him. That night I became a follower of Jesus and my life has never been the same. All too soon, the master and his disciples left our house. Mother told me that she too had been touched in a way she could not understand.

The next time I saw him, he was on a cross. I stood and watched him die, this man who had chosen me. I watched him die, this man who, without ever seeing me, without meeting me, knew that I carried more than a jar of water. In the miracle that happened for me on that day of Unleavened Bread, the miracle of Jesus choosing me from a crowded street, he took away my burden and set me free to a new life. He took my weakness and he made me strong. He took my brokenness and he made me whole.

And I am here tonight to tell you that he can do this for you, too. Amen.

What Is Truth?

by Pamela J. Tinnin

John 18:28-38

Notes

An old cleaning woman sees everything that happens the day Jesus is brought before Pilate. She never lets on that she has met the accused man before.

So, you heard about the trial? Oh, I was there all right — heard every word. I have been cleaning woman at the praetorium since the widow Riyhad died. I know everything that goes on in that place. They pay me no mind — I'm just one more widow woman.

All this craziness. I think it's just a sign of the times — things are getting way out of hand, have been a long time now. Crazy John the Baptist crying out for repentance and dunking people in the river, saying they were born again, when anyone in their right mind knows that's impossible. Always some nut claiming to be the Messiah. Conjurers and magicians in the streets, yelling themselves hoarse trying to drum up business, saying they could foretell the future, heal by a touch, or cast a spell on your enemies — after you give them a coin, of course.

I wouldn't want to be in Pilate's shoes — I mean, he's a powerful man, sets his own wages and married into money — but trying to keep the Romans happy, and convince the Jews they never had it so good. And that wife of his — well, she can't be easy to live with. Always nagging him with those dreams — dipping into the wine too often, I say.

And if he didn't have troubles enough, they went and arrested that Nazarene. Pilate tried to wash his hands of him. He thought he took care of it when he sent the Jew on to Herod, but they don't call Herod "The Fox" for nothing. Here Jesus stood before Pilate again, smelly, unshaved, in rags, looking the worse for wear ...

What is it about this Jesus? He didn't even try to fight back, just stood there quiet, trying to rub some feeling into his arms where the leather bindings pulled tight. Pilate's not a patient man. He blurts out, "So you're King of the Jews?" And then that answer — "My kingship is not of this world." Then Pilate snorts, "So you are a king?" You don't get much past Pilate, that's for sure. Then another answer that just didn't make sense: "You say I am a king — but I came to bear witness to the truth."

Then they just stared at each other for the longest time, that Jew without a hope in the world of walking away from this kind of trouble, and Pilate, probably hoping against hope that the man in front of him, reeking of blood and sweat and muck, would disappear in a puff of smoke.

Nobody moved, or said a thing. A big blow fly up near the ceiling buzzed loudly and slowly in the heat; the clop of horses' hooves sounded through the window; and still the Jew stood there, scuffing one bare foot in the dust, and saying nothing. The carpenter held his ground, kept looking Pilate right in the eye. And Pilate ... he turned away first. I almost didn't hear what Pilate said at the last; it wasn't much more than a whisper, "What is truth?" And you know, he sounded almost sad.

The truth? Pilate had the power, and Jesus had nothing. We all knew how it was going to end from the beginning. It would have taken a miracle, and though some said the carpenter had done miracles, there weren't any that day. There were plenty who wanted his blood, even in the synagogue, you could see that. He must have stepped on some pretty important toes.

I don't think Pilate cared one way or another. He isn't a bad sort, least no worse than any other prefect, as long as you stay out of his way. As my man Caleb used to say, "You've got to go along to get along."

Pilate tried to set Jesus free. The high priests didn't have enough to convict him. But, no, they wouldn't have it, and Pilate gave in. Now it's just a matter of time — they'll crucify him for sure.

There's something I haven't told anyone. Can you keep a secret? You look like I can trust you. I didn't say anything when they brought him in, but I recognized the Nazarene right off. I met him once before. It was an early morning, three years or so ago, before I came to Jerusalem to be near my son. I went down to the shore like I used to when the fishing was good. I could usually pick up a bit of work mending nets. They'd give me fish, enough to dry and to sell for a few coins.

That's when I saw him, talking to those two boys of Zebedee's, James and John they're called. The three had built a little fire with some sticks of driftwood, a big fish with its tail curling up cooked over the flames, the fat sizzling and popping when it dripped into the fire. There was the first glimmering of light at the far shore, the sun just beginning to come up, trying to shine through one of those thick Galilee fogs. The waves lapped at the rocks, knocking the boats against each other. These old bones hurt with cold, and I was shivering. The stranger waved me over, saying, "Sit by the fire, sister." He made room, then broke off a piece of the bread he was eating, and handed it to me, with a smile like none I've ever seen on any man.

Bread never tasted so good, and the fish was smoky and rich on my tongue. You could tell Zebedee's sons couldn't believe he'd called a woman to sit and eat and talk with them. But the strange one acted like it was natural as anything. At first I was too nervous to speak, but he asked me about my people, my village.

Once I started, it was like I wanted to tell it all — how when I was a girl I could run like the wind; how I haven't seen my daughter since she married that boy from the south; how funny it was that Caleb and I'd come to love each other even though our folks arranged the marriage; how much I miss that old man. The stranger ate, stirred the fire, and listened like he had all the time in the world, like my life was as important as anyone's. Talking, I forgot the cold; I forgot my worries.

When it was time to take the boats out, he filled my basket with fish, then helped me to my feet. As I turned to walk away, he stopped me. I felt the calluses on his hand as he touched my forehead, smelled the fish on his breath as he whispered words of a blessing. I watched the three of them step into the water and walk toward the boats, the dark water moving up their legs, the heavy net carried on their shoulders. The sun was up; the fog had disappeared. The Nazarene turned his head and looked back at me, and the strangest thing — his face seemed filled with light, even though it was in the shadows.

I never saw him again, not until they brought him into the praetorium. I'd heard the stories about him — I mean, the whole countryside was talking, but I kept telling myself it wasn't the one I met that morning by the sea. I'd only seen him that once, and when I remembered what happened that morning — the eating, the talking, the blessing — I began to think maybe it wasn't real — just the dreams of an old woman's heart.

"What is truth?" Pilate asked, and well he might. I think he'll come to regret the day he washed his hands and gave him up to that mob. As for the rest of us, we who don't have the courage to stop it, we who stay quiet in our corners, hoping no one notices us — we should be on our knees praying that God doesn't rend the heavens and shake the earth, and destroy us all at the moment of Jesus' dying.

Oh, I'm just an old woman — maybe my mind's going — it happens. But ... what if he is who they say? Lamb of God, Prince of Peace, Redeemer ... Messiah? In these times, it's dangerous to talk of such things, but ... could it be? Is it him? Has he really come?

I Have Seen The Lord!

by Bass M. Mitchell

John 20:1-18

Notes
Mary Magdala as the first witness to the resurrection.

My name is Mary. Many call me "Mary Magdalene" or "Mary of Magdala," for I grew up in the fishing village of Magdala on the west coast of the Sea of Galilee.

My name, "Mary," comes from the Hebrew word "Marah," which means "bitter." So my name literally means, "Bitter one."

And the name was a fitting one for much of my life. In fact, for a long time I had no life at all. Everyone said I had demons, seven of them. I do not remember that time very well. All I know is I felt complete powerlessness and hopelessness for so long.... And then, he came to our village, came to Magdala, and nothing has been the same for me since then. His name was "Jesus" of Nazareth, the son of a carpenter and some said a teacher and healer. Oh, but he was much more.

In many ways he seemed like just a normal man. Yet, there was something about him. It was in his eyes, a power, a love that looked right into my soul. But it was his voice that touched me the deepest, a voice of such power yet gentleness. When he spoke, healing and wholeness for the first time came into my life. He set me free and at the same time enslaved my heart, for my heart from that moment on would be his.

I became his disciple, you see, following him with many others throughout Galilee. And I heard that same, wonderful voice continue to bring healing, hope, and sweetness into my life and the lives of so many others. Oh, the stories I could tell you. But I must hasten to tell you what happened over the last week.

As we made our way to Jerusalem, I sensed in him a deep sadness. As we approached the city, I saw him standing on a hilltop and that wondrous voice of his saying, "Jerusalem, Jerusalem, the city that kills the prophets and stones those who are sent to it! How often I have desired to gather your children as a hen gathers her chicks under her wings, and you were not willing...."

And I saw the tears streaming down his face....

I felt the tears stinging my own eyes, too, at his pain. And my heart was frightened, afraid of his words then and afterward, for he spoke of how he was going to die. I did not understand him. No one did. No one believed such a thing could happen to him. Not now. Not in the holy city. Surely this could not be.

Oh, the last traces of bitterness fled my heart on that joyous day we entered Jerusalem. I think you call it "Palm Sunday." Everyone greeted him with singing and shouting, "Hosanna! Blessed is he who comes in the name of the Lord!" I knew something wonderful was about to happen....

How quickly things changed....

I saw him cast the moneychangers out of the Temple. I didn't understand why, but I knew it made the leaders angry. I heard their whispers; I saw them plotting against him. I began to fear for him.

Then, sometime on Thursday night, all my fears became reality, for news came that he had been arrested. How could this be happening? It had to be a mistake. Surely they would see this and release him. If only they had asked me, I could have told them about him. I could make them see in him what I and so many others saw. But they would never listen to a mere woman. They would not allow me anywhere near him. And some of the old bitterness and powerlessness began to creep back into my heart....

What was happening? Why was it happening?

I was there when Pilate brought out Barabbas and Jesus. I could not hold back the tears as I saw him standing up there, bruised, beaten, a crown of thorns around his head. Pilate asked the crowd, "Who do you want me to release to you — Barabbas or Jesus?"

I cried out, "Jesus!" with all that was within me, but it was a whisper in a thunderstorm as the crowd shouted, "Give us Barabbas! Crucify Jesus!"

"Crucify Jesus?" How could anyone dare speak such a thing? How could this be happening?

I watched in horror as Pilate washed his hands and gave the order for Jesus to be crucified....

Deep down I wanted to run away. It was more than I could endure. The other disciples, even Peter, who said he'd die with Jesus, had denied him and fled at the last. But I could not.

I watched as they placed the heavy crossbeam on his back and led him through the streets of Jerusalem. My heart broke anew into a thousand pieces when I saw him fall on his face beneath its weight. I was powerless once again ... so useless. The demons had returned.

I stood as close as they would allow me when the procession finally stopped outside the city walls. Golgotha. I hated that place. I looked up and saw the three stakes already in the ground. Roman stakes. Why had God allowed those pagans to conquer us? And why would God allow my Lord to be led to such a fate as this?

Oh, the bitterness filled my heart and mind then. A bitter numbness came over me as I saw the soldiers lay him on the ground. The pounding of the nails through his wrists sent waves of pain through my heart. He was then raised and fastened to the stake, a nail driven through his feet. A sign placed over his head, "This is Jesus, King of the Jews." The soldiers gambled for his only piece of clothing. And people shouted for him to save himself. Wasn't it enough that he was dying? Did they have to mock and curse him, too? I hated them bitterly.

Then I heard that voice again, this time as the soldiers and others cursed him ... "Father, forgive them, for they know not what they do."

But I could not forgive them. The bitterness was too great.

Then his voice reached my ears again, as he spoke to one of the thieves ... "Today, you will be with me in paradise."

Then I heard him speak to Mary, his mother, and to John.

Of John he said to his mother ... "He is now your son."

Of Mary he said to John ... "She is now your mother."

And then I heard what I thought was bitterness in him as he cried out ... "My God, my God, why have you forsaken me?"

"God had forsaken us all," is all I could think and feel.

Then, in a whispery, dry voice he said ... "I thirst."

And I wasn't even able to do anything about that.

And finally, the last words I knew I would ever hear him speak ... "It is finished ... Father, into your hands I commend my spirit."

And his voice was silent. I would never hear it again....

I followed Joseph of Arimathea and Nicodemus as they took his body down and placed it in a garden tomb not far from Golgotha. We had to hurry for Sabbath began at sunset and they had to be finished before then.

For the rest of that Friday night, and all of Saturday, I could not sleep or eat. Finally, I arose well before dawn on Sunday morning and decided to go the garden tomb. Perhaps, if I was literally closer to him, even though he was dead, it would give me some peace of mind, some relief from the bitterness and grief.

When I reached the tomb, I knew immediately that something was wrong. The great stone that I had seen several men roll in front of the tomb had been rolled aside. In fear, confusion, and anger, I ran back to Jerusalem and awoke Simon Peter and John.

And in trembling voice I told them, "They have taken the Lord's body from the tomb and I don't know where they have put him!"

Wasn't it enough that they crucified him! Did they also have to desecrate his body? New bitterness filled my heart again.

All three of us raced back to the tomb. John and Peter both went inside. They said they only saw the linen burial cloths resting on the rocky ledge on which Jesus' body had been laid. The clothes were not torn or in disarray but lying there as if the body of Jesus had simply passed right through them.

I was too upset to even go inside the tomb. Peter and John came out, confused and bewildered. They went back to the city. I stayed. I was alone again. And I began to cry.

Suddenly, something told me to look inside the tomb. I did and I saw two beings in white sitting at the head and foot of the place where Jesus was laid. They asked me, "Woman, why are you weeping?"

"They have taken my Lord away, and I do not know where they have put him!" I said through my tears. And suddenly they were gone. I must have been seeing things. Was I going mad again?

Then I became aware of a presence behind me. I half turned and glanced at him through my tears, thinking he was the gardener. The man asked me, "Woman, why are you crying? Who are you looking for?"

"If you took him, sir," I answered, "tell me where you have put him, and I will go and get him."

Then, in the quiet morning stillness of the first Easter, I heard, "Mary!"

"Mary," the voice said again.

That voice. I knew that voice. That voice knew me.

And I realized somehow that it was Jesus standing there with me. And my first thought was that I was going mad after all.

"Mary," he said tenderly again.

"Rabboni," I managed to whisper, which means "My Master" or "My Teacher."

"Mary," he said, looking at me. I would know his eyes, his voice anywhere. I was not mad. He was there! He was alive!

I had thought I would never hear him say my name again. He was alive! And he called my name, "Mary!" That voice, that one word brought a flood of sweetness back into my soul, washing away all the bitterness, pain, anger, and grief. He had set me free again. This time, forever.

And he told me to go and tell his friends that he was alive and that he would meet them in Galilee. I did not wish to leave him, but did as he commanded. I found them and shouted with all the joy in me, "I have seen the Lord!"

And they did not believe me, not until they, too, saw him.

This is my hope, my prayer for each of you this Easter. That this very day in this place, or in your own garden, or even in the midst of your own bitterness and grief, you will hear the Risen Lord speak your name.... For the Risen Christ knows you, loves you, too.

So, listen for your name. I don't know how, when, or where it will come. But he will call your name. You will encounter him. And listen for the task he has for you. Then go and share with joy, "I have seen the Lord!"

The Early Church Grows

Rock The Boat!

by Bass M. Mitchell

John 21

Notes
A conversation between the disciples while in a boat.

Maybe I should not read the Bible just before I go to sleep at night. "Why?" you ask. Because I have a tendency to dream about whatever I read. Take this story from John 21:1-14. I read it recently and found myself in a dream out there on another boat watching and listening. Here's what I saw and heard....

The disciples of Jesus had gone back to the same old boats, their fishing boats, that is. And apparently they had even forgotten how to do that, for they had fished all night and not even caught a minnow or a bass! Suddenly, a voice came out to them across the water from a man standing on the shore: "You haven't caught anything, have you?"

Thomas shouted back, "No, we haven't."

I saw Nathaniel squinting his eyes and looking in the distance. "Who is that, anyway? I can't quite make him out from here," he said.

James looked too. "Don't know," he said.

"But that voice sounds familiar," the one named John replied.

And then the voice came again: "Try casting your nets on the other side. You'll catch some fish there."

This time the large one named Peter looked toward the shore and said, "Who does that guy think he is, Jesus? What does he know about fishing? We're the fishermen here."

James replied, "Yeah. We practically grew up on this lake, didn't we? No one knows it better than we do."

"Yeah, lots of good memories on this old lake. I especially remember that one day, don't you?" John asked.

Then Peter said what they are were thinking, "How could we forget that day? It seems so long ago now ... we were fishing like today when another man came to the shore...." (Peter's words were lost in silence for a moment and I could tell he and the rest of them were greatly moved.)

John continued for him ... "And this man, this strange, wonderful man spoke such wondrous things. He told us to follow him and he would make us fishers of people."

"But we didn't understand then, did we?" James asked.

"But we left our nets and our boats and followed him anyway," Peter added. "Who would have ever thought it would have ended that way? A cross! I feel as empty as these fishing nets."

And that voice came echoing again over the water to them: "Cast your nets on the other side of the boat."

Nathaniel said, "I don't know. I'm tired. Why bother? Let's just pull the nets up and call it a day. Besides, I'm feeling just a little seasick and don't think I can take anymore rocking of the boat."

But the voice still echoed: "Cast your nets on the other side of the boat."

"But, we've never done it that way before, you know, fished over there. Everyone knows you can't catch fish over there," James said.

Thomas replied, "But what do we have to lose? I know it's a lot of work and we're probably wasting our time. But what else have we got to do? It's sure not working on this side."

The other disciples gave reluctant grunts of agreement. They hauled in the nets, rocking the boat back and forth as they moved around, then let the nets out on the other side. They had hardly placed the nets in the water when I heard Peter say, "Well, I'll be! Look at that."

And I saw them all bending over looking at their nets. Thought they were going to turn the boat over! And even from where I was sitting I could see that their nets were teeming with fish, swelling their nets until it seemed they would burst! Then John looked toward the shore again, a look of light and hope on his face. I heard him shout, "It's the Lord!"

And all the disciples then looked and knew it, too. Peter was so excited that he jumped into the water and swam to shore. For such joy had filled their hearts again, a joy even greater than that first day when he had called out to them. The others tugged on the nets, heavy with fish, and eventually came to shore, where, sure enough, Jesus greeted them and had breakfast ready. And I saw them eat together, the weariness and emptiness replaced with new strength and purpose.

Suddenly I found myself on the shore with them and they began to speak to me.

Nathaniel spoke first. "Sometimes, my friend, you just can't keep doing things the same old way, fishing from just one side of the boat."

"That's right," Thomas joined in. "Sometimes you have to do something different, even if you doubt it will work."

"Change positions. Rock the boat a little," John added.

James said, "Yeah, make some waves."

"Yes, even seasoned fishermen can still learn something new," Peter said.

Then I heard Jesus say to me: "Rock the boat! Cast your nets on the other side!"

Lord, you know I don't much like rocking the boat, making waves. Getting out of a rut is just too bumpy. What's that, Lord? "A rut is just a grave with the ends knocked out?" If you say so, Lord. I'll give it another try. Show me where to cast my nets and hand me some seasick medicine. Amen.

Even The Gentiles

by Peter K. Perry

Acts 10 and 11

Notes

Simon of Joppa gives his testimony before the Council of Elders. This message is a bit of my imagination based on the story of Peter's appearance before the Council of Elders in Jerusalem after the conversion of Cornelius, the Roman centurion upon whom the Spirit of God descended. I believe that Simon of Joppa was there in Jerusalem, corroborating the testimony of Peter before the council. This is his testimony.

You have asked me to testify before you, the Council of Elders, as to the events surrounding the conversion of Cornelius, a centurion in Caesarea. So I will tell you what happened there and what is happening still wherever Christians proclaim the story of Jesus.

My name is Simon of Joppa. I am a tanner by trade and I have been a follower of the way and a disciple of Jesus for many years. I heard him preach once and saw in him then a power and presence and a truth that I had never seen before. I guess you could say I became a believer. In those days there was no church to join and no creeds to recite. If you loved Jesus, if you believed his message, if you named him Lord, then you were a follower of the way. You were still welcome in the synagogue. You were still a Jew. Jesus wasn't about dividing people ... he was about uniting people. All of the divisions that we know today came later, much later.

I was born and raised a Jew and I have always honored my past and worshiped the God of Abraham, Isaac, and Jacob. My heart thrills to read the words of Joshua, "As for me and my house, we shall serve the Lord our God," or to say in the synagogue, "My father was a wandering Aramean," or to celebrate my heritage as a member of the tribe of Benjamin. None of that was supposed to change when I began to follow Jesus. After all, Jesus was a Jew.

But not long after Jesus' death and resurrection, the leaders of the synagogue began to criticize the followers of Jesus. I, and other followers of Jesus, began to grow uncomfortable. It was a hard time to be a Jew. And it was a hard time to be a follower of Jesus. We weren't sure who we were or where we belonged. We still went to synagogue services. But we began meeting in the homes of other believers as well.

And the world was rapidly changing around us. Rome was hell-bent on destroying the last vestiges of Israelite independence. The ways of the Romans and the Greeks were becoming more and more acceptable. Every community was experiencing foreign immigration. In the marketplace you heard Greek spoken as often as Aramaic. Young Jewish men were marrying Gentile women and Jewish girls were taking Gentile husbands. Old values were giving way to new ideas, and many among the Jews didn't like it ... didn't like it one bit. Maybe that's why we followers of Jesus were meeting so much opposition. We were seen as the radicals, the troublemakers, and the ones with the crazy new ideas who were trying to change everything that was holy. I remember hearing one elder of the synagogue say, "Well, this Jesus may have been a Jew, but he ate with Samaritans and Greeks, so you can't trust him or his followers!"

But, despite the lack of acceptance among the leaders of the synagogue, the circle of believers continued to grow. God's Spirit touched more and more people with the excitement of faith. The numbers of those who were saved through that faith in Christ was growing daily. The growth among the Christians only further alienated the believers from the old guard. But despite the strained feelings, we followers of Jesus still understood ourselves to be Jews. And most of us believed that to be a Christian you had to be a Jew first.

That's the way things stood that day when Peter was staying at my house. I was outside working when Peter called to me. "Simon," he shouted, "come quickly!" So I came. It was Peter after all, the leader of the twelve, the big fisherman who, led by the Spirit, had done so much already to share the teachings of Jesus.

It was an honor to have him spending a few days at my house as he rested from his journeys.

"What is it, Peter?" I asked.

"Simon, I've had the most unusual vision...."

And then he told me the story that has become so infamous, the story of the sheet lowered from heaven, filled with all the animals, clean and unclean alike. I will never forget the story of the vision or the excited way Peter told it ...

"I looked in the sheet and I saw the animals ... there were sheep and goats, oxen and swine, horses and lions, snakes and lizards, fishes and birds, insects and rodents ... I'm telling you, Simon, it was a menagerie. In my vision, I was wondering what all of this was about when the voice of God spoke to me saying, 'Peter! Kill and eat!'

" 'No way, God!' I said. 'I'll take the sheep and the goats, but all of those other animals in there are unclean ... unfit for human consumption ... a disgrace to the laws of Moses ... a dishonor to you, great God!' But God said, 'Do not call anything impure that God has made clean.' "

While Peter was considering that, God spoke again. Again God said, "Kill and eat!" So Peter reminded God again ... "Hey, God," Peter said, "you gave us rules about these things. Don't you remember? We're not supposed to eat these kinds of animals." But again God replied, "Do not call anything impure that God has made clean."

A third time God said, "Peter! Kill and eat!" And a third time Peter said, "No." "What is this, God," Peter asked, "some kind of purity test? Well, I won't ever eat anything unclean. I am a Jew and I will live by the rules of our ancestors, the law of Moses. So God, did I pass the test?" And God said a final time, "Do not call anything impure that God has made clean."

Peter said to me, "Simon, I was filled with a great sense of sadness as the sheet filled with all of the animals was raised back up into heaven, and I knew that if this had been a test, I surely failed. God is doing a new thing, Simon. God is doing a new thing!"

Just as Peter said this, a strange expression came over his face. He looked at me and said, "Simon, three men are approaching, looking for me. Go welcome them, care for their needs, and tell them that I will be ready to travel with them tomorrow."

"Who are they, Peter?" I asked.

"I don't know, Simon, but the Spirit has told me to go with them. Come with me, Simon, and bring some of the brothers, too."

So I went downstairs and welcomed the strangers and gathered some of the believers. The next morning we traveled together to Caesarea, to the home of Cornelius, a Roman centurion in whose heart God had been working. Cornelius was a good man, who prayed to his gods and did many works of charity, but make no mistake about this: Cornelius was as good a Roman as I was an Israelite. He worshiped his pagan Gods as surely as I worship Yahweh. He followed his Roman ways as closely as I followed the laws of Moses. Cornelius was no Jew. Cornelius was a Roman. Yet, Cornelius had been sent a vision from God, our God, the one true God. God told Cornelius to send for Peter so that Peter might teach him of Jesus.

Peter stood outside, in the courtyard of Cornelius' house, and prayed. God was asking him to do a new thing. God was asking Peter to share the Good News with a Gentile, a non-believer, one who was unclean. The brothers from Joppa and I watched in amazement as Peter broke every rule and stepped into the house of Cornelius, prayed with him, ate with him, even laughed and played with his children, for Cornelius' entire family had assembled there. Following Peter's lead, we, too, went in and served God in the house of a pagan.

A most amazing thing happened as Peter preached there and told the story of God in Jesus to this family of Romans. Just as it had done in the Upper Room, just as it had done with many of the believers among the Jews, the Holy Spirit of God came down and rested on Cornelius. I know! ... I know ... that cannot be ... but it happened nevertheless. Cornelius received the blessing of God and his heart was filled with Jesus as surely as mine and yours have been filled. Peter looked at me in amazement and said, "God's Spirit has come *even* to the Gentiles! Simon, do you see? God is doing a new thing."

"Yes, Peter, he is!" I said, "He most certainly is!"

So that's what happened, most learned Council. And this is the way I have come to understand the meaning of it all. Just as Jesus has come to be known as the bridge between God and humankind, so too Jesus has become the bridge between peoples ... between the Jews and the Gentiles, between the slave and the free, the black and the white, the man and the woman. Jesus told us that message again and again while he was with us, but we did not understand. And sometimes we still fail to understand. God is doing a new thing. I believe that God will always be doing a new thing. Whenever and wherever we, in our frail human wisdom, proclaim that one person is a child of God and another is not, Jesus will come and tell us we are wrong. For God has the power to proclaim the impure clean. And God's Spirit will blow in the most amazing places!

So, yes, brothers and sisters, an unbelievable thing happened that day when Cornelius and his family became the first Gentile followers of Jesus. But I don't believe that they will be the last. Cornelius is a good man, and I for one believe that God was working in his heart long before he ever heard of Jesus or Peter or a Council of Elders in far-off Jerusalem. You must know that's the truth! You know there are many good people like Cornelius and his family who are not believers. They don't look like us. They don't talk like us. They don't live like us or follow our customs. But they are children of God, nonetheless. And we are called to love them and to offer them the faith that has so filled our lives with meaning and purpose, and yes, even salvation. We are not called to judge them, for judgment belongs to God. We are called only to embrace them as brothers and sisters in God's family.

I know that in all times and all places this will be a stumbling block for believers like you and me, for it is hard to imagine that God can be so inclusive when our human instincts lead us to make distinctions and divisions. And so we must always remember this story of Peter's vision of the clean and the unclean, and the word that came from God to Peter, in my home, in the house of Simon of Joppa; "Do not call anything impure that God has made clean."

Onesimus

by Peter K. Perry

Letter To Philemon

Note

Onesimus, the once runaway slave of Philemon, who became a co-worker with Paul, tells his story.

Hello. My name is Onesimus, Bishop of Ephesus. We bishops spend so much time dealing with the administrative tasks of the church, and the controversies that spring up almost daily, that we rarely get an opportunity like this one. Preaching to you today reminds me of the old days. You see, I wasn't always a bishop. Before God blessed me with this calling to be the shepherd of the Ephesian Church, I was just a preacher. And before that ... yes, before that, I was just a slave. I was just a slave.

I was born into the household of Philemon of Colossae, my master. My mother had lived her entire life as handmaid to our mistress Apphia, wife of Philemon. She died soon after my birth, and so nursemaids raised me alongside the master's son, Archippus. My father worked in Philemon's fields, though I rarely saw him. My early childhood in Philemon's house was blissful. I would play all the day long with Archippus, who was just a year younger than me. Once we were old enough to escape the watchful eyes of the nurses, we would escape the house to roam the hills around Colossae. From some of the higher ones we fancied that we could see the vastness of the great sea to the south, or the great city of Ephesus, a fortnight's journey to the east. Colossae itself was situated in the Lychus Valley, near the headwaters of the Meander River. Since it was on the busy road that the merchants used to carry their goods west to Greece and east to Antioch, the city was always an exciting, bustling place. On days when Archippus and I weren't exploring the hills, we were usually exploring the city and, more often than not, getting into a great deal of mischief.

Officially, I was a manservant for Archippus, but I enjoyed a great deal of freedom, going everywhere he went, doing everything he did. Sometimes I felt as though I was not the son of my father, but of Philemon, for I was treated with much respect by all of the other slaves in the household. Often, when Archippus received a gift from his father, I too would enjoy some token. Growing up with Archippus, even though I was in reality a slave, was a very easy life, and one that I enjoyed immensely. I looked forward to every day.

Well, every day except the Sabbath, that is. Archippus felt the same way. We dreaded the Sabbath. Philemon, you see, had got religion. He was the leading member of a group of Greek Jews who worshiped a man named Jesus. I didn't understand what all the fuss was about. Once a week, all of these Christians, as they were beginning to call themselves, would gather in the great hall of my master's house to share a meal and sing hymns. After singing, someone would preach about this man Jesus. Rarely did they have anything exciting to say, however. As members of the household, we all had to go to these gatherings. Since they were the same every week, I took to sleeping through them. After the meal, that is!

One week, just before Archippus turned twelve, a visitor came through Colossae on his way to Ephesus. All of the Christians were excited about the visitor. For once, the Sabbath was different. We still shared the meal and sang the hymns, but afterward this stranger, whose name was Paul, talked all afternoon and into the night. Needless to say, I fell asleep right away. I guess I just wasn't interested in what he had to say. Things certainly changed a few short months later. Little did I know then that one day soon Paul would hold my life in his hands. Had I known then what I know now, I would probably have tried to pay attention to Paul's words. Instead, I slept through the Sabbath as I did every week, and when I woke up the next morning, Paul had already left for Ephesus.

Soon thereafter, Archippus reached his twelfth year. Philemon arranged for him to have lessons from the Academy at Colossae.

His studies would take all of his time, and so I would no longer be needed to keep him company. Overnight, I went from enjoying the privileges of being Archippus' companion to being a common, ordinary slave, working beside my father in Philemon's fields, wearing calluses into my hands that had never known hard labor.

Being a field hand was very different from enjoying the privileges of being valet to a boy. I was awakened before the rising sun and worked hard until there was no light to see by in the evening. I ate cold meals in the fields and slept in the slave quarters. There were no more gifts from the master. Worse, there was no longer the look of respect in the eyes of the other slaves.

As if this sudden change in my status in Philemon's house were not bad enough, shortly after I began working in the fields, my father grew sick. In a week he was dead. With both my mother and father gone, with Archippus at the academy, there was nothing to keep me with Philemon — except of course the small fact that I belonged to him. I was tired of working in the fields. I wanted my freedom again, as I had known it growing up with Archippus.

Brothers and sisters, what I did next is not pleasant for me to recall. I decided to run away, to seek freedom and fortune in Ephesus. But worse, I knew that I would need money, and so I stole from the treasury of Philemon. I took gold, silver, and jewelry — not too much, but enough to support me for a time in the city. Yes, I, Onesimus, Bishop of Ephesus stole from my master! The memory pains me still, and it shall pain me always. But when I did this terrible deed, I felt no pain at all. I was as yet blind.

I will not bore you with the details of my experiences in Ephesus. Suffice it to say that they resembled those of the Prodigal Son, which our Lord described. I squandered the stolen gold and silver, sold the stolen jewelry, and squandered the money it brought. All this time I lived in fear of my life that I would be found out. For the law of the empire says that the master of a runaway slave has the right to put the slave to death if he so desires. So I kept a low profile. I had to take questionable jobs from people who would hire a person with no history. They didn't ask questions of me and I didn't tell tales on them.

I couldn't afford to buy food. I stole when I could and ate from garbage when I couldn't. I slept in alleys. I came to realize that life had been better as a field hand in the household of Philemon. Oh, yes, then I had been forced to follow orders and work long hours, but at least I ate regularly and slept in a bed. I had traded my life in Colossae for a dream of freedom. But I had been freer as a slave than I was as a runaway. Now I lived in constant fear. Oh, to go back to my former life, but it was too late to go back!

Such was my state of mind the day I saw the stranger who had spoken that Sabbath in Colossae. I could hardly believe that it had only been six months earlier when I had slept through his preaching. Paul was his name. When I saw him, the authorities were arresting him. It seems he had incited a riot by preaching against the graven images and idols the townspeople worshiped. People were listening to Paul, and the metal workers who made the idols feared for their jobs. They started the riot, but Paul was the one who got arrested. They called it protective custody since the authorities were afraid of Paul. He was a popular man and a Roman citizen. Locking him up in house arrest did restore calm to the city, and though Paul couldn't leave his room, his friends could come and go as they pleased. It effectively kept Paul quiet and kept him from doing much preaching about Jesus.

Maybe it was only my imagination, but as I watched Paul being arrested, I thought our eyes made contact and I saw the glimmer of recognition in his. Could he have remembered me from Philemon's house? I felt haunted by that image of his eyes. Were they beckoning to me? Did he know who I was, what I had done? Did he know how I was living in the shadows, how much I regretted having run away? Did he know what a fool I had been? I agonized over that haunting moment for days. I wanted to go to him, but I was afraid. He might turn me in, but on the other hand, I couldn't go on living as I was. It was only a matter of time until my past caught up with me. At last, I decided to see him, and that was the second most important decision of my life.

I went to the house where he was being held. When I had been admitted, Paul greeted me ... by name! He had noticed my slumbering that night in Colossae, and he asked for my name so that he might pray for me, that I might awaken to the message of his master Jesus.

Paul asked me how I came to be in Ephesus without my master. Despite my fears, I poured out the story of my frustration in Colossae, my fallen ways in Ephesus, my fears of being discovered, and of facing my punishment. When I was finished, Paul just looked at me for a few moments, and then he spoke.

"Onesimus, you desire freedom. You have abandoned your master, you have stolen, and you have lived as a criminal lives — all in search of freedom! Truly, Onesimus, the freedom you seek is already yours. You must simply accept it. Look at me! Am I not free? Has not Jesus Christ made me free? Think about this, and come back tomorrow. I will speak with you again."

How could Paul say that he was free? He was under arrest, guarded day and night! Intrigued, I returned the next day, and the day after, and every day for a fortnight. Paul told me stories of Jesus and freedom, stories I had heard before, but never listened to, stories that now took on new meaning. One day, Paul told me that my chasing after freedom was like running a race.

"Surely you know, Onesimus, that many runners take part in a race, but only one of them wins the prize. Run then, Onesimus! Run in such a way as to win the prize. It is not the prize of being free to come and go as you please. It is not the prize of great wealth and earthly power. No, Onesimus, run for the prize of freedom in Jesus Christ! Run for the finish line that you might find your freedom in him."

I told Paul that I wanted to run that race, that I wanted that freedom. I called Jesus my Savior that day and when I did, I felt free — freer than I had been when lying in the sun in the hills about Colossae together with Archippus, freer than when I was newly arrived in Ephesus with Philemon's money. For the first time in my life I was truly free. Letting Jesus into my life was the most important decision I ever made!

There still remained the problem of Philemon. I was still a runaway slave, and a thief to boot. But Paul had an answer to that also. The very next day, when I went to visit Paul, he wrote a letter on my behalf to Philemon, the contents of which you are no doubt familiar. He explained all that had happened in Ephesus, and how he had found me. He told me he would intercede on my behalf, and folding the letter, he sealed it. I took the letter, and Paul's blessing, and I returned to Colossae.

Of course, when Philemon received me, he was threatening the worst. But as he read the letter from Paul, his mood changed and he began to smile.

"Onesimus," he said, "truly in Christ there is neither Jew nor Greek, neither slave nor free. The freedom you have found far exceeds the freedom I give you today. Consider yourself forgiven and return now to Paul, as he has need of you in Ephesus."

And so I did just that. I was with Paul until the end, my knowledge and faith growing in his presence. By association with him, I became Bishop of Ephesus. And yet, strangely my fame is not from my episcopal office, but from my bondage and my liberation through the love of Jesus.

That, friends, is the story of my life. That is my testimony. The events I've described happened a long time ago, and I have lived far more than my share of years. I've seen much in all of the years, but of all of my experiences, of all the stories I could tell you today, this one is my favorite. For in Jesus Christ, I found my freedom.

About The Authors

Pamela J. Tinnin was the pastor of Partridge Community Church (United Church of Christ), the only church in Partridge, Kansas (population 250). She recently moved to northern California, where she is helping rear some real sheep. Prior to her graduation from Pacific School of Religion in Berkeley, California, Tinnin was an editor for ten years with the University of California-Berkeley. She has also been the editor of a small-town newspaper, a freelance writer, a sheep rancher, a paralegal working with prison inmates, a small-town city clerk, and a migrant worker in the fields of Oregon.

Peter K. Perry has been the senior pastor of First United Methodist Church in Phoenix, Arizona, since July 2001, and has previously served churches in Prescott, Sedona, and Mesa, Arizona. He currently chairs the Board of Ordained Ministry for the Desert Southwest conference of the United Methodisti Church, and also writes for *Emphasis* preaching journal. Perry is a graduate of California State University, Fullerton (B.A. in history) and Pacific School of Religion in Berkeley, California.

Bass M. Mitchell serves as a United Methodist minister in the beautiful mountain area of Hot Springs, Virginia. He is a prolific writer who has contributed several hundred articles to various publications, including *Homiletics* and *Circuit Rider*. Mitchell regularly writes devotions for *The Upper Room* and *Upper Room Disciplines*, as well as Bible studies and other curriculum for the United Methodist Publishing House. He is the author of *God Sightings: Discovering God in Everyday Life* and *In Every Blade of Rustling Grass* (Abingdon Press).

www.ingramcontent.com/pod-product-compliance
Lightning Source LLC
Chambersburg PA
CBHW071717040426
42446CB00011B/2111